40 Days of

Missional Living

A 40-Day Spiritual Growth Campaign

"40 Days of Missional Living"
Encouraging words to the reader...

I love hearing stories of churches that have caught the vision for what it means to live "on mission." But for a church to reach that point, each individual member must live missionally as well. By participating in this campaign, you have the opportunity to be a part of seeing First Baptist Church Mount Sterling go to the next level of missional activity. Imagine how God will work in your community and around the world through that kind of church.
Kevin Ezell, President of the North American Mission Board, SBC

To be like Jesus is to be on mission. I am so encouraged that you are walking through '40 Days of Missional Living' together and believe that this could be a powerful tool that God uses to shape you into Jesus' image, and to redeem many people through faith in Jesus Christ. I hope you will take seriously the content of this campaign as it seeks to help your church more effectively fulfill the Great Commission.
Micah Fries, Former Vice President of the LifeWay Research and current Senior Pastor of Brainerd Baptist Church in Chattanooga, TN.

Jesus established His church on earth for a reason and that reason is the Great Commission. Fulfilling the Great Commission is THE MISSION of a biblically faithful church. I'm certain that God will use "40 Days of Missional Living" to help First Baptist Church Mount Sterling be even more focused on that mission and even more effective at taking the gospel to the nations.
Paul Chitwood, Executive Director of the Kentucky Baptist Convention

Jesus' last command on earth was for His church and disciples "to go." Go with a message, mission, and purpose. It is exciting to see that you as a church family will be focused on better understanding the Church's commission: The Great Commission. As a result of what God does in each of your lives individually as well as in your church as a family, you could be part of a movement of God that shakes and shapes your community for decades to come. Be prayerful, be responsive, and most of all be obedient. May the Lord fill your hearts with passion, open doors of opportunity, and allow you to bear much fruit for His glory as you take this 40-day journey together.
David Stokes, Executive Director of the Central Kentucky Network of Baptists

Just go! That's the command of the Great Commission to all believers. "40 Days of Missional Living" is an excellent resource to help believers see that we can be on mission wherever the Lord plants us to serve Him.
Donnie Fox, President of Clear Creek Baptist Bible College

Living out the Great Commission is certainly a purpose worth pursuing with passion. I am thrilled to hear that First Baptist Church Mount Sterling is taking this unique opportunity to focus on Jesus and His mission for 40 days. I am confident this commitment will result in a spiritual harvest beginning within the congregation and reaching around the world, just like Jesus did.
Shannon Benefiel, Former Dean at Clear Creek Baptist Bible College and current Associate Pastor of First Baptist Church Millington, TN.

Table of Contents

40 Days of

Missional Living

Section One: Spiritual Growth Campaign

Spiritual Growth Campaign
Contributors

Jason Bratcher is a member of First Baptist Church Mount Sterling and serves on the worship team. He graduated with a Bachelor of Arts from the University of Kentucky where he majored in Philosophy and Computer Science. He also completed his Master of Divinity (M.Div.) in Theology at Liberty Baptist Theological Seminary with a 4.0 GPA. Jason is a licensed Minister of the Gospel (2002). He is married to Katie Bratcher.

Garrett Collier serves as a Worship Ministry Intern at First Baptist Church Mount Sterling. Garrett also serves on the FBC Missions Board. He is pursuing a Bachelor of Arts in Ministry from Clear Creek Baptist Bible College. Garrett is married to Sofia Collier and they have three children: Zhayda, Ayden, and Aramis.

Chris Dortch serves as the Lead Pastor of First Baptist Church Mount Sterling. He graduated Summa Cum Laude (4.0 GPA) from Liberty University with a Bachelor of Science in Religious Studies (Theology and Biblical Studies). He also completed his Master of Divinity (M.Div.) and Doctor of Ministry (D.Min.) degrees from Liberty Baptist Theological Seminary. Pastor Chris is also a licensed (1995) and ordained (2000) Minister of the Gospel. He is married to Cheryl Dortch and they have one son, Carson. Carson and his wife Jessica live just north of Charlotte, North Carolina.

Charlie Holder serves as the Student Pastor of First Baptist Church Mount Sterling. He graduated from Liberty University with a Bachelor of Science and holds a Master of Arts in Religion (M.A.R.) with emphasis in Discipleship and Church Ministry from Liberty Baptist Theological Seminary. Pastor Charlie is a licensed Minister of the Gospel (2015). He is married to Sarah Holder.

Austin Lewis is a member of First Baptist Church Mount Sterling. He holds a Bachelor of Business Administration in Finance from Morehead State University. He is currently pursuing a Master of Divinity (M.Div.) in Christian Ministry from The Southern Baptist Theological Seminary. Austin is married to Makayla Lewis.

Kris Mann is a deacon of First Baptist Church Mount Sterling and serves on the church's Mission Board. He holds a Bachelor's degree in Business Administration from Alice Lloyd College and a Master's degree in Juvenile Justice Studies from Eastern Kentucky University. Kris is a licensed Minister of the Gospel (2016). He is dating Kayla Daulton and enjoys spending time with his family and fishing.

David Tevis is a member of First Baptist Church Mount Sterling and serves on the church's Visioneering Team. He holds a Bachelor of Science in Education from Asbury University and a Master of Business Administration from Morehead State University. David assisted with proofing and editing. David is married to Margaret Tevis.

Jordon Wade serves as a Student Ministry Intern at First Baptist Church Mount Sterling. He is pursuing a Bachelor of Arts in Ministry from Clear Creek Baptist Bible College. Jordon is dating Makenzie Shrout and enjoys personal evangelism.

Christopher Wilson serves as the Worship Pastor of First Baptist Church Mount Sterling. He graduated from Wright State University with a Bachelor's degree in Music. He is currently pursuing a Master of Divinity (M.Div.) through Liberty Baptist Theological Seminary. Pastor Christopher is a licensed Minister of the Gospel (2005). He is married to Naomi Wilson and they have two children: Clara and Henry.

Spiritual Growth Campaign
Overview and Commitments

Over the next 40 days we will be focused on deepening our understanding of living out the Great Commission. Through weekend worship services, small group studies, and the daily devotions and journal, the entire church will focus on the Great Commission for 40 days! Imagine the impact of our entire church focused intently on living out the Great Commission for a period of 40 days. Each person devoted to spending time in God's word and time in prayer and then intentionally seeking to live out the Great Commission on a daily basis. Undoubtedly, individuals will grow in their faith. Our church family will be better equipped to fulfill the Great Commission. Our families will be strengthened. Even our community will benefit from our growth! This is the type of unity that Paul wrote about in Philippians 2:2, "Fulfill my joy by being like-minded, having the same love, being of one accord, of one mind."

There are three major commitments of this spiritual growth campaign.

1. **Individual Commitment** (Daily Devotions & Journal)
   This campaign is designed to help you develop and strengthen your daily time with the Lord in His word and in prayer. Each day, you will read a brief devotion, followed by a point of application (Salt & Light) and a closing biblical thought or principle (One Last Thought).

2. **Small Group Commitment** (Sunday School or Home-Based)
   One of the powerful elements of the spiritual growth campaign is encouraging one another through authentic biblical community called "small groups." Whether your small group is Sunday School Based or Home Based, it is essential to the "40 Days Spiritual Growth Campaign" to commit to a small group for the six weeks. The small group aspect provides an environment for discussion, application, and accountability. Through our time in small group, we hope you will be encouraged, you will grow in your faith, and our church will be unified in love, spirit, and purpose as together we search the Scriptures! You can visit the "40 Days Information Table" in the lobby to commit to a small group during the 40 days campaign.

3. **Large Group Commitment** (Weekend Worship Services)
   Each Sunday of the spiritual growth campaign, we will focus on a particular aspect of the Great Commission and discover personal application. There is no need to sign up, just show up!

Spiritual Growth Campaign
Campaign Leadership Team

Lead Pastor: _____

The Lead Pastor will give spiritual leadership to the campaign, casting vision, and motivating the congregation to get involved.

Campaign Director: _____

The Campaign Director works closely with the Lead Pastor and manages the coordinators in making sure everyone has the resources they need. The Campaign Director can usually be found at the "40 Days Information Table" in the lobby each Sunday.

Prayer Coordinator: _____

The Prayer Coordinator is not only praying for the success of the spiritual growth campaign, but is concerned with involving others in prayer for the campaign. If you would like to join the Prayer Team for the spiritual growth campaign, please visit the "40 Days Information Table" in the lobby.

Evangelism Coordinator: _____

The Evangelism Coordinator will give oversight to the "40 Souls" project. Our desire is to reach 40 souls with the gospel during the 40 days spiritual growth campaign. If you would like to participate in this soul-winning project, please visit the "40 Days Information Table" in the lobby.

Small Group Coordinator: _____

The Small Group Coordinator/Coach will be responsible for recruiting, training, and equipping all small group leaders during the campaign. If you have questions about hosting, leading, or joining a small group, please visit the "40 Days Information Table" in the lobby.

Worship Coordinator: _____

The Worship Coordinator will assemble a creative team to gather ideas and then work together in planning and implementing the thematic worship services during the campaign. If you are interested in being part of this creative team, please visit the "40 Days Information Table" in the lobby.

Children & Student Coordinator(s): _____

The Children & Student Coordinator(s) will be responsible for coordinating all children and student involvement during the campaign. If you are interested in more information about children and student involvement, visit the "40 Days Information Table" in the lobby.

Spiritual Growth Campaign
Small Group Leadership Team

Small Group Coach (Also a member of the Campaign Leadership Team)
The Small Group Coach oversees all of the Small Group Leaders within a particular type of small group (e.g. Children, Students, Sunday School-Based, and Home-Based). The Small Group Coach has three primary roles.

1. Huddle: Meet regularly with your small group leaders to pray, train, and equip. Always make sure that your small group leaders have the resources they need.
2. Visit the Group: Visit each small group at least twice each year to affirm the leader and the group.
3. One-on-One: Make personal contact with each small group leader and seek opportunities to shepherd them.

Small Group Leader
The Small Group Leader provides personal leadership to their small group. There are six primary roles of the small group leader.

1. Prepare the lesson and facilitate discussion. As soon as you receive the material, review the lessons and become familiar with the "big idea" of each lesson. Prepare your mind for leading your small group.
2. Select at least one apprentice and possibly two apprentices to train and give opportunities to lead.
3. Shepherd your small group by helping them develop Spiritual HABITS and movement in spiritual growth.
4. Meet with your Small Group Coach on a regular basis.
5. Attend huddle meetings with your Small Group Coach for prayer, training, and equipping.
6. Guide the group toward reproduction of another small group within 18-24 months.

Small Group Apprentice
The Small Group Apprentice is being prepared for the role of Small Group Leader. It is the understanding that they will launch their own small group within 18-24 months and develop their own apprentice(s). There are six primary roles of the apprentice.

1. Identifies, welcomes, and introduces guests.
2. Takes attendance and reports to the SG Coach.
3. Makes preparations for and opens the group with an icebreaker or topic-teaser.
4. Ensures a refreshment schedule is developed.
5. Leads the discussion/teaching time once each month.

6. Leads the group in developing a group mission project (if the group does not have a Small Group Missions Coordinator).

Small Group Host (Home-Based Groups)
The Small Group Host is primarily concerned with creating a welcoming environment. There are six primary roles of the Small Group Host.
1. Provides a location for the group to meet.
2. Arrives early and greets everyone as they arrive.
3. Sets up refreshments at least 15 minutes before the meeting time.
4. Arranges the chairs for best small group interaction.
5. Sets the temperature around 70 degrees.
6. Make sure pets are put away.

Additional Small Group Leadership Opportunities
The small group environment can be a great place for providing every individual in the church with some ministry role. It will ensure that our church does not operate with 20% of the people doing 80% of the work. Here are some additional ideas for members of your small group. Your small group may come up with many other leadership roles not listed here.
1. **SG Prayer Warrior:** Organizes and communicates prayer requests.
2. **SG Spiritual HABITS Champion:** Provides resources and accountability for those in the group developing spiritual disciplines.
3. **SG Refreshments Coordinator:** Develops the refreshments schedule for the group.
4. **SG Missions Coordinator:** Oversees the logistics and communication of SG mission projects.
5. **SG Childcare Coordinator:** Develops the childcare schedule for the group.
6. **SG Ice-Breaker Coordinator:** Makes preparations for and leads the weekly icebreaker or topic teaser.
7. **SG Card Coordinator:** Responsible for sending out cards to the group (e.g. we miss you, get well, happy birthday, etc.).
8. **SG Fellowship Coordinator:** Responsible for logistics and communication of SG fellowship events.
9. **SG Worship Leader:** Responsible for leading worship songs/hymns during your small group gathering.
10. **SG Social Media Coordinator:** Responsible for managing social media page(s) for SG activities and communication.

Spiritual Growth Campaign
Resources

There are numerous resources that have been developed for this spiritual growth campaign. We hope that you will familiarize yourself with each of the tools available to you!

1. **40 Days of Missional Living Devotional & Journal**
   You're holding it! This book will be your guide over the next 40 days. Additional books are available at the "40 Days Information Table" in the lobby. You can also visit www.40days.cc for other options. Here are some of the components of the devotional and journal and how they can help you deepen your walk with the Lord over the next 40 days:
   - **Scripture Verse:** Each devotion begins with a verse of Scripture that you can meditate on throughout the day. You could even develop the spiritual discipline of Scripture memory.
   - **The Devotion:** The devotion provides a brief understanding of the Scripture passage through commentary and application.
   - **Salt & Light:** This section provides you with a brief prayer or action step to move you toward application of the biblical truth.
   - **One Last Thought:** The "One Last Thought" is often a short synopsis of each day's devotion. It provides a summary of the biblical truth as a closing thought.
   - **Journal:** There is space with each day's devotion to write down your own personal thoughts on what God is teaching you. Your retention for learning is increased when you write things down in your own words, even if you never look at it again!

2. **40 Days of Missional Living Small Group Guide**
   You're still holding it! This book also contains your small groups lessons. There is no difference between the leader's guide and participant's guide. It is all one "small group guide" in which participants can follow along with the facilitator's notes. While the daily devotions are for your individual walk with the Lord, the Small Group material will serve as a guide for prompting discussion among a small group of believer's over the next six weeks.

3. **40 Days of Missional Living Audio Book**
   The daily devotions are also available in audio format on CD. Whether you are "on the go" or simply need audio assistance, this resource will help you keep up with the daily devotions.

4. **40 Days of Missional Living Scripture Memory Key Tags**
    The Scripture memory key tags are another way to meditate upon God's word. There are 18 verses printed on a plastic tag to easily carry with your keys. For more information about the Scripture Memory Key Tags, visit www.40days.cc.

5. **40 Days Spiritual Growth Campaign Website**
    Here you will find information about this and other 40 days spiritual growth campaigns. As the spiritual growth campaign progresses, we may have new ideas and resources that we will make available here: www.40days.cc.

Spiritual Growth Campaign
Spiritual HABITS

We want every member of our small groups to be developing spiritual disciplines that will help them grow on their own. As you have no doubt experienced, there are some awesome things God does in the lives of His children when we "take a break" from the busy-ness of life and draw near to Him. Learning some classical spiritual disciplines won't just enhance your maturity; your growth will not be dependent on a program. To help members of every small group develop these disciplines we have developed some resources. It would be good for every Small Group Leader to know what the HABITS are and to practice them in your own life as you encourage your small group to do the same. While this is not an exhaustive list of spiritual disciplines, they are foundational to the Christian faith and serve as a starting point for spiritual growth.

Hang Time with God
Description: Daily time in prayer and reading God's Word.
Resource: 40 Days of Missional Living

Accountability in a Small Group
Description: Small Groups provide a relational community for discussion, application, and accountability of the Christian faith.
Resource: Small Group

Bible Memorization
Description: Memorizing and meditating on God's Word.
Resource: Scripture Memory Key Tags

Involvement in Ministry & Mission
Description: Actively serving in the church as well as actively involved in missions. Every believer has a ministry in the church and a mission in the world!
Resource: Where do you serve?

Tithing Commitment
Description: Stewardship over God's resources. This discipline is about giving regularly and generously with a cheerful heart to the local church.
Resource: The Stewardship Challenge

Sermon Application
Description: Making personal application of weekly sermons.
Resource: Ask, "What does God want me to do in response to 'hearing the word'?"

Spiritual Growth Campaign
Research

Research conducted by the Barna Group in 2017 revealed that over half of active United States churchgoers have never even heard of the Great Commission! Here are the startling results of the research...

Churchgoers: Have you heard of the Great Commission?
- No. (51%)
- I'm not sure. (6%)
- Yes, but I can't recall the exact meaning. (25%)
- Yes, and it means... (17%)

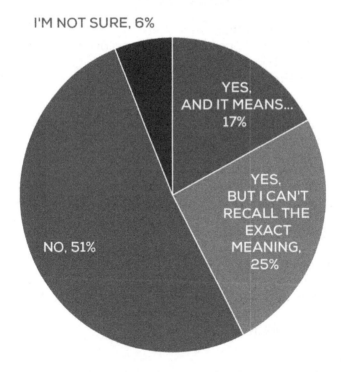

CHURCHGOERS: HAVE YOU HEARD OF THE GREAT COMMISSION?

Barna

I'M NOT SURE, 6%

YES, AND IT MEANS... 17%

YES, BUT I CAN'T RECALL THE EXACT MEANING, 25%

NO, 51%

October 2017, n=1,004 U.S. churchgoers.   © 2018 | barna.com

DO CHURCHGOERS RECOGNIZE THE GREAT COMMISSION AMONG OTHER VERSES?

Barna

"Go and make disciples of all nations, baptizing them in the name of the Father and of the Son and of the Holy Spirit, and teaching them to obey everything I have commanded you." (Matthew 28:18-20)	37%
"'Love the Lord your God with all your heart and with all your soul with all your mind,' This is the first and greatest commandment. And the second is like it: 'Love your neighbor as yourself.'" (Matthew 22:37-40)	16%
"I am the way and the truth and the life. No one comes to the Father except through me." (John 14:6)	8%
"Whoever wants to be my disciple must deny themselves and take up their cross and follow me." (Mark 8:34)	5%
"Give back to Caesar what is Caesar's and to God what is God's." (Mark 12:17)	2%
Not sure if any of these passages are the Great Commission	33%

October 2017. n=1,004 U.S. churchgoers.   © 2018 | barna.com

[1]Barna Research Group. "51% of Churchgoers Don't Know of the Great Commission." Barna.com. https://www.barna.com/research/half-churchgoers-not-heard-great-commission/ (accessed July 13, 2018).

40 Days of

Missional Living

Section Two: Devotions, Journal, & Small Group Guide

Introduction

The Great Commission is simply the biblical command of Christ to carry and proclaim the gospel to all nations. The Great Commission is not strictly a New Testament concern. As we discover in the Old Testament, it has been God's plan all along. Isaiah 45:22 carries the idea of taking salvation to the ends of the earth, "Look to Me, and be saved, all you ends of the earth! For I am God, and there is no other." It is clear that God desired to bless Abraham and his descendants for the purpose of being a blessing to all the families of the earth (cf. Gen. 12:3).

The "40 Days of Missional Living" devotions are built around the Great Commission statements as recorded in Matthew, Mark, Luke, John, and Acts. Each book provides a unique perspective into accomplishing the Great Commission.

The *goal* of the Great Commission is to make disciples. Matthew's account of the Great Commission emphasizes the goal. For this reason, we must have a solid biblical understanding of what a disciple looks like.

The *method* of the Great Commission is to preach the gospel. Mark's account of the Great Commission emphasizes the method. The preaching of the gospel is essential to accomplishing the Great Commission.

The *message* of the Great Commission is the gospel and focuses on the incarnation of Christ, His death, His resurrection, and His return. Luke's account of the Great Commission emphasizes the message. It is important to understand the themes of the gospel and the core content of the Good News.

The *authority* of the Great Commission is from God the Father. John's account of the Great Commission emphasizes the authority behind it. Jesus was given all authority and He has commissioned us with this great task.

The *strategy* of the Great Commission is to expand the Kingdom of God. Luke provides tactical strategy through the Book of Acts in how we are to accomplish this God-sized task.

There are three things we hope to accomplish through *40 Days of Missional Living*. First, we hope to encourage your personal walk with Christ. We desire for these devotions to be an encouragement to your faith journey of missional living. Second, we hope the local church is strengthened and empowered by the Holy Spirit to make a Kingdom impact. We believe the local church is part of God's strategy to accomplish the Great Commission. The local church should be a group of like-minded believers who have covenanted together to accomplish the Great Commission. Third, we hope to encourage your impact on the community in which you live. The idea of missional living is that believers are called to live on mission within the community in which God has placed them. God has placed you where you are to bring the peace of God to the city (cf. Jer. 29:7).

I am looking forward to discovering how the Lord will challenge us as a church over the next 40 days as we strive to live on mission!

Exodus 19:5-6,

Pastor Chris Dortch

"A great commitment to the Great Commission and the Great Commandment will grow a great church." –Rick Warren

"We must be global Christians with a global vision because our God is a global God." –John R.W. Stott

"The gospel is only good news if it gets there in time." –Carl F.H. Henry

"You have one business on earth – to save souls." –John Wesley

"I'm not afraid of failure; I'm afraid of succeeding at things that don't matter." –William Carey

"As long as there are millions destitute of the Word of God and knowledge of Jesus Christ, it will be impossible for me to devote time and energy to those who have both." –J.L. Ewen

"We talk of the second coming; half the world has never heard of the first." –Oswald J. Smith

Week 1

Matthew: The Goal

This week we will focus on Matthew's account of the Great Commission and the goal of making disciples. Therefore, everything we do as a church should be about making disciples. This week we will discover that each of the five purposes of the church play a role in making disciples.

"And Jesus came and spoke to them, saying, 'All authority has been given to Me in heaven and on earth. Go therefore and make disciples of all the nations, baptizing them in the name of the Father and of the Son and of the Holy Spirit, teaching them to observe all things that I have commanded you; and lo, I am with you always, even to the end of the age.' Amen."
Matthew 28:18-20

Day 01:
Making Disciples

Matthew 28:18-20, "And Jesus came and spoke to them, saying, 'All authority has been given to Me in heaven and on earth. Go therefore and make disciples of all the nations, baptizing them in the name of the Father and of the Son and of the Holy Spirit, teaching them to observe all things that I have commanded you; and lo, I am with you always, even to the end of the age.' Amen."

Matthew's account of the commission is the most well known version of the five, and the one commonly referred to as *The Great Commission*. Each version of the Great Commission has its own unique emphasis and purpose. In Matthew, the emphasis is on the goal of our commission: making disciples.

Before proceeding, it is important to make a distinction between making disciples and making converts. The two are not the same; making converts, leading people *to* Christ, is only the first step in a lifetime commitment. Making disciples means not only introducing people to Christ, but also partnering with those same people to become people who live by Christ's teachings and seek to reproduce by making more disciples.

Examining the New Testament, we find five elements necessary to make healthy disciples: worship, fellowship, discipleship, serving, and missions. Worship directs people toward God and allows them to praise Him. Fellowship connects people to fellow believers allowing them to share their struggles and spiritually support one another as they grow in their faith. Discipleship increases spiritual knowledge and strengthens believers to overcome the obstacles the world puts in their way. Serving allows believers to humble themselves and create opportunities for others to be loved and introduced to Christ. Missions allows believers to share what Christ has done for them with others in order to grow the kingdom of God. Short of implementing all

Journal:

five elements, we are failing to achieve God's commission because all of them are necessary.

This means everything the church does is about making disciples. In fact, if something isn't about making disciples, the church has no reason to do it. When we allow other things to become our focus, we are only creating obstacles to the gospel. The biggest obstacle to the gospel is not Satan. It is not science. It is not atheists. It is not Islam. It is Christians! Many Christians are concerned more about worldly things than about spreading the gospel. Consider these distractions:

- When Christians allow themselves to become concerned more with comfort than reaching their neighbors.
- When Christians allow themselves to care more about tradition than caring about the lost world around them.
- When Christians allow themselves to be known for what they are against rather than what they are for.
- When Christians are more concerned about making their opinion heard than allowing Christ's voice to shine through them.
- When Christians spend all their time arguing among themselves about things that have no eternal significance instead of maintaining unity in the Spirit.
- When Christians are concerned more about what others think of them than about the word of God.

We must be diligent to keep our eyes focused on Christ and the mission that He has entrusted to us. If we allow the distractions mentioned above to creep in, we risk God removing His hand from our church. God is going to accomplish His purposes one way or another. We should desire to join Him in His work.

SALT & LIGHT: Ask God to show you what distractions you have allowed to hinder you from accomplishing the Great Commission and what you need to do to get on board with God's plan for His church.

ONE LAST THOUGHT: We cannot neglect any part of the discipleship process described in Scripture or allow distractions to hinder the task, as our lost neighbors are depending upon us to share the gospel with them.

Day 02:
Making Disciples: The Importance of Worship

Acts 2:46-47, "So continuing daily with one accord in the temple, and breaking bread from house to house, they ate their food with gladness and simplicity of heart, praising God and having favor with all the people. And the Lord added to the church daily those who were being saved."

Journal:

_____
_____
_____
_____
_____
_____
_____
_____
_____
_____
_____
_____
_____
_____
_____
_____
_____
_____
_____
_____
_____
_____
_____
_____
_____

It should come as no great surprise that worship and making disciples are of ultimate importance for the church. The two, however, are sometimes seen as entirely distinct portions of what the church does. One of the reasons for this is that we are often prone to compartmentalize these aspects of our faith. This means worship becomes something that we do for thirty minutes on Sunday mornings and discipleship is reserved for the church leaders and pastors. Unknowingly, we tend to reduce the importance of both in the lives of each and every follower of Christ.

Worship, in a broad sense, is our response to God's glory, goodness and love. The word most often translated as worship in our Bibles carries a more specific meaning of bowing before a king. With this in mind it is important to remember that worship and obedience are closely related. Worship is not simply singing or music, but rather it happens, or should happen in all aspects of our lives. We worship when we pray. We worship when we sacrifice. We worship through our generosity. We worship through our love. We worship through our service. Worship is not an act in which we engage, but it is the very foundation upon which our faith is built. When we worship we are bowing before and being obedient to our King.

Discipleship is similar in many ways. Imagine for a moment that you were to remove all aspects of discipleship from the New Testament. If you were to eliminate the commands and commissions and the actual accounts of Jesus' leading of His disciples, what would be left? We cannot reduce the Great Commission to something that is merely a small aspect of Christianity. It *is* Christianity. Likewise, we must never think that discipleship is something that only the pastor is responsible for. If you are a Christian, you are a disciple and you are also called to make disciples!

When we reduce the scope of worship and discipleship, a division between the two inevitably occurs. If, however, we begin to give worship and discipleship the magnitude of attention that they require, we begin to see that making disciples is one of the most worshipful things that we can do. Theologian and preacher, Charles H. Spurgeon went so far as to say to his students "Our great object of glorifying God is to be mainly achieved by the winning of souls." We might be tempted to think that the church, as mentioned in the passage above, grew simply because they continued to meet together and praise God. What is clear, though, is that their worship was not isolated to these times that they met with one another. The book of Acts provides a wonderful model that shows the early church worshiping continually by fulfilling the Great Commission. God added to their number, not only because they joined together, but also because when they weren't together their focus was still on bowing before their King by creating disciples.

SALT & LIGHT: God help me to worship You more fully. Help me not to reduce the most important aspects of my faith to things that only happen on Sunday mornings. Help me to continuously bow before You by living out the Great Commission each day.

ONE LAST THOUGHT: One cannot create disciples without worshipping and one cannot worship without creating disciples.

Day 03:

Making Disciples: The Importance of Fellowship

Acts 2:42, "And they continued steadfastly in the apostles' doctrine and fellowship, in the breaking of bread, and in prayers."

Journal:

_____
_____
_____
_____
_____
_____
_____
_____
_____
_____
_____
_____
_____
_____
_____
_____
_____
_____
_____
_____
_____
_____
_____
_____
_____

Making disciples is more than just telling people about Christ and making converts. Just giving ascent to Christ and increasing spiritual knowledge is not enough to make someone a disciple. To be a disciple means a commitment to and a relationship with Christ. In fact, this point is implicit in Matthew's account of the Great Commission in a number of ways.

First, an interesting element of Matthew's account is the absence of the ascension. From the other versions of the commission, we know that Jesus returned to heaven shortly after giving the disciples their marching orders. However, Matthew emphasizes Jesus' continuing presence with His disciples by leaving the ascension out. In fact, this is one of Matthew's primary themes throughout the gospel (cf. 1:22-23). This is because our mission as a church depends upon Jesus' presence with us here and now.

Second, the original Greek makes it clear that God intends a relationship with believers. However, we frequently miss this point because of English. The "in" is translated from the Greek word εἰς, which is closer in meaning to "into." This implies a much deeper connection than simply saying "in." "In the name" implies an association; "Into the name" implies entering into a relationship. We are being baptized into the eternal relationship that God the Father, God the Son, and God the Holy Spirit have always shared with one another. Through our relationship with God we have access to His authority, mercy, grace, peace, and love; only with access to God can we accomplish our task.

Third, our commission doesn't end with baptism. If it did, we could potentially make the argument that our job is done once someone accepts Christ and is baptized. However, Christ commanded us to come alongside the new believer and teach them all things that Christ taught and commanded. Once they are baptized into a relationship with God, we are called to establish a relationship with them as well and help them grow in their faith.

Solomon tells us, "Though one may be overpowered by another, two can withstand him. And a threefold cord is not quickly broken" (Ecc. 4:12). The life of a disciple takes a three-part relationship between the believer, God, and the church (other believers). Unfortunately, the church often fails believers and lets them slip away without ever aiding them in their spiritual growth. While there is great power in God's word (Scripture), by divine design, it is not enough to transform the world without the church (other believers) to proclaim God's word. Otherwise, the church would be unnecessary and we would immediately be called home once we accept Christ. In a fallen world, we need others to support us or we would be so beaten down by daily life that we would quickly fall away (cf. Matt. 13:20-21). We need relationships with others to grow in our faith; iron sharpens iron (cf. Prov. 27:17). Therefore, we need additional ministries beyond Sunday morning to provide social support. This is why fellowship and enjoying the company of other believers is so important to the health of a church and successful missional living. We need fellowship meals; we need youth theme nights; and we need hula-hoop classes. We need as many opportunities to cultivate good relationships as possible. It's not about the activity, it's about the relationships that are made and strengthened through those activities that are important.

SALT & LIGHT: Think back for a moment, what do you remember the most: Sunday morning messages or spiritual conversations with close friends sitting in your home? It's the times and conversations we spend in fellowship with others that stick with us over the years and make the biggest impact on our lives.

ONE LAST THOUGHT: Saying, "I don't need church - I study the Bible for myself" is proof that you don't actually study the Bible for yourself.

Day 04:

Making Disciples: The Importance of Discipleship

2 Timothy 2:2, "And the things that you have heard from me among many witnesses, commit these to faithful men who will be able to teach others also."

Paul's second letter becomes more personal when he encourages Timothy to continue the ministry in his absence. Paul's 2 Timothy 2:2 focus continues his 1:13 point, telling us to hold on to the pattern of sound teaching. Paul then emphasizes how we are to follow that pattern in 2 Timothy 2:2. Paul tells Timothy that the many witnesses could testify to the soundness of the teaching as truth from God. Believers are called to share the gospel once they have received the gospel themselves. More importantly, believers are called to do this faithfully.

Faithful men have practiced 2 Timothy 2:2 throughout history because they knew its importance. They also understood they could not let the gospel die with them. Think about it this way: Paul's message went from a hole in the ground in Rome to where you are reading this devotion two thousand years later. These men, over the years, found faithful believers who could do the same through discipleship. Discipleship requires building relationships with time, vulnerability, and trust. These three things tend to push believers away from making disciples because of what it requires. In response, many believers abdicate their personal disciple-making responsibility to the pastor. However God calls us all to make disciples (cf. Acts 1:8).

There are a few things that we can learn from Paul and his relationship with Timothy that will help us as believers make disciples and train other believers for the gospel. The first is careful observation. Believers must look for others to disciple who can then make other

Journal:

_____
_____
_____
_____
_____
_____
_____
_____
_____
_____
_____
_____
_____
_____
_____
_____
_____
_____
_____
_____
_____
_____
_____
_____
_____
_____
_____
_____
_____
_____

disciples. It also requires relationship development. We must be meeting regularly, ministering together, and going to conferences. The great example is that Paul took Timothy with him. He did not just hand him a "how-to book". Additionally, discipleship involves coaching. Believers must help by teaching and leading others in areas of sharing the gospel and developing godly character.

Jesus references this in Luke 6:39-40 when He poses the question: "Can the blind lead the blind? Will they not both fall into the ditch?" He then gives an answer to this question in verse 40: "A disciple is not above his teacher, but everyone who is perfectly trained will be like his teacher." Jesus tells us that as believers we should be leading the blind out of darkness and into the light, but we should not leave it at that. We should then teach them how to lead others out of the darkness and we should train them how to grow in their faith by leading them. We can observe the Paul/Timothy model of discipleship as our example.

SALT & LIGHT: God, show me someone today that I can disciple. Show me someone that I can train to teach Your word to others. God give me the knowledge of Your word so that I can do this effectively in Your name. Amen.

ONE LAST THOUGHT: As believers, we are called to make disciples of those that are in our church and community. Therefore, we must build relationships and teach them how to make disciples of others.

Day 05:
Making Disciples: The Importance of Ministry

Ephesians 4:11-12, "And He Himself gave some to be apostles, some prophets, some evangelists, and some pastors and teachers, for the equipping of the saints for the work of ministry, for the edifying of the body of Christ."

"Ministry" is one of those words that is often misused in church life. We have a tendency to label just about anything as a ministry. It comes from the Greek word "diakoneo" which means, "to serve." Therefore, the biblical usage and understanding of the word is associated with serving the needs of others. Unfortunately, many in our churches want to know what ministries are offered to them. This is in complete contrast to Jesus' model of ministry where He came, not to be served, but to serve.

Ephesians 4:11-12 reminds us that while God has called some to equip, He has called all believers (i.e. saints) to the work of ministry. When we are all serving, the church is then edified. Furthermore, the Bible teaches that the Holy Spirit gives all believers at least one spiritual gift when they are saved. Whether you have one spiritual gift or many, your spiritual giftedness is needed for the entire church body to function properly. In fact your spiritual gift is not for your own benefit, but for the benefit of others.

Take some time to complete the Spiritual Gifts Inventory found on page 169 in Appendix C. As we come to the realization that all Christians are called to do the work of ministry, we should seek to know how God has gifted us and reflect upon how those gifts are building up His church!

SALT & LIGHT: Complete the Spiritual Gifts Inventory in Appendix C and identify your top three spiritual gifts. Once you have identified

Journal:

_____
_____
_____
_____
_____
_____
_____
_____
_____
_____
_____
_____
_____
_____
_____
_____
_____
_____
_____
_____
_____
_____
_____
_____
_____
_____
_____
_____

your top three gifts, start using them in your church! Don't wait to be asked, the biblical mandate is to use the gifts God has given you, not wait until someone asks you to use them!

ONE LAST THOUGHT: The church will never reach their full potential in accomplishing the Great Commission without you exercising your spiritual giftedness in ministry!

Day 06:

Making Disciples: The Importance of Missions

Romans 10:14-15, "How then shall they call on Him in whom they have not believed? And how shall they believe in Him of whom they have not heard? And how shall they hear without a preacher? And how shall they preach unless they are sent? As it is written, 'How beautiful are the feet of those who preach the gospel of peace, Who bring glad tidings of good things!'"

Don't you find it hard to believe that the all-knowing God of creation entrusted His plan of salvation to fallible humans? Yet, that is exactly what He did. Before Christ ascended into Heaven He gave the disciples instruction to carry the Good News of salvation to the entire world. He gave that instruction to a group of men who were full of imperfections, all of whom had denied and abandoned Him just weeks before! Why would He do such a thing?

God's ways are truly higher than our ways. Somehow, He is able to see straight through to the heart of men, to their innermost being. He knew that those same men who had failed Him, and then experienced His amazing grace, would become the most committed and genuine spokespeople the world would ever know. Who could make a grander witness to others in need of the salvation than those who have partaken of His divine love and goodness firsthand?

From the beginning, God has had a plan to redeem sinful man back to Himself through His son Jesus. God has been on mission since the beginning and He calls us, as born again believers, to join Him. We are to be about the mission of telling the world that Jesus Christ saves! Without our participation, souls will forever be lost. Each of our salvation experiences should remind us of the same grace that the Disciples experienced and spur us on to missional living.

Journal:

Scripture tells us that even the angels rejoice over one lost soul coming to repentance. If God gave His very own Son because of His great love for mankind, He certainly wants the world to know. Will you join Him in that mission? Will your feet deliver the gospel of peace and glad tidings of good things?

SALT & LIGHT: God, please send workers into Your harvest fields. Give us the strength and boldness to share Your glorious gospel message around the world. Make me Your missionary.

ONE LAST THOUGHT: God has been on mission since the beginning and He calls us, as born again believers, to join Him.

Day 07:

Making Disciples: The Mount Vision

Matthew 28:19-20, "'Go therefore and make disciples of all the nations, baptizing them in the name of the Father and of the Son and of the Holy Spirit, teaching them to observe all things that I have commanded you; and lo I am with you always, even to the end of the age.' Amen."

This week we have examined the goal of the Great Commission, "to make disciples." We have discovered that discipleship is not isolated from worship, fellowship, ministry, or missions. Instead, these purposes are woven together to fulfill the Great Commission. The word "disciple" is used more than 270 times in the New Testament. Through these passages we see the recurring commitments of what it means to be an authentic Christ-following disciple.

The first commitment of a disciple is sacrificial. The starting point of this commitment is at the disciple's moment of salvation. The new believer has made a decision to submit to Christ and surrender their will and to follow Christ no matter what the cost. Sacrifice of time, energy, body, and even future plans are all understood to be part of this commitment to come after Christ. In his book *The Cost of Discipleship*, Dietrich Bonhoeffer states, "When Christ calls a man, he bids him come and die." What makes this sacrificial call so difficult is that we are called to sacrifice our own desires for our enemies. It is easier to make sacrifices for those we love, but the call of Christ demands a sacrifice far more reaching. Submission to Christ and His plan is the highest goal for the disciple.

The second commitment of a disciple is relational. Love is the hallmark of followers of Christ. If I love God then I want to spend time with Him and His children. Love for God, love for neighbor, and love for other disciples is an essential part of the value system of a disciple.

Journal:

_____
_____
_____
_____
_____
_____
_____
_____
_____
_____
_____
_____
_____
_____
_____
_____
_____
_____
_____
_____
_____
_____
_____
_____
_____
_____

The authentic disciple will set aside time to be with other Christians for spiritual nourishment and encouragement. They also prioritize serving the body by discovering their spiritual gifts and using their giftedness to serve Christians and non-Christians alike. The local church is the focal point for this relational community and service.

The third commitment of a disciple is transformational. The purpose of spiritual growth is directed toward becoming like Christ in word, thought, attitude, and action. Spiritual disciplines such as Bible study, journaling, Scripture memorization, prayer, fasting, and tithing are all means to an end. They connect us to the grace of God and through the grace of God we are transformed into the image of Christ. As we become like Christ in character, we also become more committed to the cause of Christ. Being leads to doing. This disciple is transformed in their character and calling. In Philippians 3, the Apostle Paul wants to know Christ, the fellowship of His sufferings, and the power of His resurrection. Paul wanted to have an intellectual and experiential knowledge of Christ! He also wanted to "press on" and accomplish the work that he was called to do. This type of transformation connects the disciple to the person of Christ as well as the mission of Christ. You cannot be a follower of the person of Christ without being a follower of the mission of Christ.

As we continue this 40-day journey, may these three principles of what it means to be a disciple help de-mystify what an authentic disciple looks like.

SALT & LIGHT: Think back over the past few months. What have you sacrificed for the sake of following Christ? What relational role are you taking to help the church "make disciples"? How are you continuing to be transformed into the image of Christ?

ONE LAST THOUGHT: Missional living flows from a disciple who is making sacrificial, relational, and transformational commitments.

Small Group Guide for Week 1: **The Goal**

WELCOME: If your group is new or if you have new members, take time to briefly introduce yourselves.

CAMPAIGN OVERVIEW AND PRAYER: Take a moment to read through the "Spiritual Growth Campaign: Overview and Commitments" as found on page 9 to the rest of the group. Ask for a few people to share what they hope to get out of the next 40 days. As your group shares, you may want to write down some of their hopes for the campaign below. Once people are finished sharing, take some time to pray for your small group.

SHARE: What I hope to gain for "40 Days of Missional Living"...

_____

_____

_____

_____

SPIRITUAL HABITS: One of the ways we grow in our faith as Christians is by developing spiritual disciplines. To help you remember some of the basic spiritual disciplines, we use the word HABITS. Not all habits are bad. In fact, these habits are worth developing. See page 15 for a list and description of the Spiritual HABITS. Over the next 40 days, we are encouraging our church family to spend daily time in God's word and in prayer. We hope your small group will be a place where you can share your challenges and victories.

LEADER NOTE: Consider having your group form accountability groups of 3 to 5 to discuss your progress in developing Spiritual HABITS. It is best to allow groups to select accountability partners and not assign them. Scripture memory key tags are available and you may want to pick some up for your small group.

TOPIC TEASER: "Barna Research and the Great Commission"
Take a moment to review the results of Barna's research concerning the Great Commission on pages 16-17. Do these results surprise you? Why or why not?

READ THE SCRIPTURES:
Ask for a volunteer in the group to read Matthew 28:16-20. Consider reading it a few times from different translations.

STUDY THE SCRIPTURES:
What is the goal of the Great Commission?

DISCUSSION:

Use the space below to take notes on your discussion of the devotions.

_____
_____
_____
_____
_____
_____
_____
_____
_____
_____
_____
_____
_____

APPLY THE SCRIPTURES:

A passage of Scripture has a specific meaning, but has many points of application. As a group, discuss how you have been challenged to live missionally as a result of your time in God's Word this week?

MY PERSONAL ACTION STEP:

What do you think God wants you to do as a result of your studies and small group discussion this week?

_____
_____
_____

PERSONAL

MISSIONS PROJECT:

If your small group does not already have a Small Group Missions Coordinator (SGMC), please take time to choose a leader for this role. The SGMC will coordinate the logistics of all small group missions projects. They will also provide a weekly update of progress toward the mission project(s). Once you have selected your SGMC, then take some time to brainstorm a few missions project ideas that your small group can implement during the "40 Days Spiritual Growth Campaign." The goal of this project should emphasize the Great Commission. Be prepared to share possible mission projects (write some ideas below) and then make a final decision during next week's small group gathering.

_____
_____
_____
_____
_____
_____
_____

MISSIONS COORDINATOR

SNEAK PEEK:
Next week we will focus on the *method* of the Great Commission. If you did not complete the Spiritual Gifts Inventory on page 171 in Appendix C, make sure you complete it before our next small group gathering because we will take some time to talk about it.

PRAYER REQUESTS & PRAYER:
Take prayer requests and close in prayer.

_____
_____
_____
_____
_____
_____
_____
_____
_____

LEADER NOTE:
Dismiss your group, but make yourself available to anyone who has questions.

Week 2

Mark: The Method

This week we will focus on Mark's account of the Great Commission and the method of making disciples. The method of carrying out the Great Commission is through the preaching of God's Word. This week we will examine how we can preach the gospel to others and ourselves.

"And He said to them, 'Go into all the world and preach the gospel to every creature. He who believes and is baptized will be saved; but he who does not believe will be condemned."
Mark 16:15-16

Day 08:
Preaching the Gospel

Mark 16:15-16, "And He said to them, 'Go into all the world and preach the gospel to every creature. He who believes and is baptized will be saved; but he who does not believe will be condemned."

In Mark, the emphasis is on the method of delivery: preaching the gospel. The Greek word translated as preach is κηρυσσω (kerruso). It means to be a herald or to announce a message publicly with conviction. We tend to think of preaching as what the pastor does on Sunday morning. However, "preaching the gospel" means much more. For one, it is something we are all called to do, suggesting that the idea of preaching as defined by the modern context is not the whole meaning. Also, in order to announce something with conviction, our words alone are not enough.

In a world with multiple worldviews claiming to be true, it is important for us to show the truthfulness of our message. Our message is the very word of God and has the power to change the heart, "For the word of God *is* living and powerful, and sharper than any two-edged sword, piercing even to the division of soul and spirit, and of joints and marrow, and is a discerner of the thoughts and intents of the heart" (Hebrews 4:12). However, this does not mean that it is enough simply to tell people what Scripture says. People are good at identifying hypocrisy in others and if our words do not match our actions, then we do damage to our message.

"What *does it* profit, my brethren, if someone says he has faith but does not have works? Can faith save him? If a brother or sister is naked and destitute of daily food, and one of you says to them, "Depart in peace, be warmed and filled," but you do not give them the things which are needed for the body, what *does it* profit? Thus also faith by itself, if it does not have works, is dead" (Jam 2:14-17).

Journal:

As James noted, faith (or saying we have faith) without works is dead. Therefore, everything we do must reinforce and confirm our message. Only then do we show real conviction and help the message to be received with rejoicing. This is why the gospel should permeate everything we do, otherwise all we end up doing is showing others that our faith is dead and useless to change our lives in a meaningful way.

It is not that God's words are insufficient, but that the human heart needs to be softened before it will accept them. Sometimes people just need to see that the message is true and effective before they can buy in themselves. They need to see that our lives reflect what we are saying is true in order to know that it is true. So, we should think about everything we do as preaching the gospel.

SALT & LIGHT: Ask God to reveal to you how you can use your job, your hobbies, and your attitude to preach the gospel.

ONE LAST THOUGHT: The Holy Spirit uses all manner of means to break down our defenses so that we will be receptive to God's message.

Day 09:

Preaching the Gospel: Through Our Words

Ephesians 4:29, "Let no corrupt word proceed out of your mouth, but what is good for necessary edification, that it may impart grace to the hearers."

Repeatedly in Scripture, we read passages that concern our speech; it is clearly important to God how we use our words. It is through human words, both written and spoken, God has chosen to reveal Himself to the world. Recall the inspiration of Scripture. How is it that God's revelation comes to us? 2 Peter 1:21 says, "For no prophecy was ever produced by the will of man, but men spoke from God as they were carried along by the Holy Spirit (ESV)." Simply put, God's word comes to us through men who were inspired by the Holy Spirit. Though the canon of Scripture is closed, God continually works through the preached word as the glorious gospel of Jesus Christ is proclaimed. Thus, the words we speak each day should be chosen with great care, as our mission is to make Christ known.

As we consider Ephesians 4:29, it is important that we grasp the context in which it was written. The immediate context (v. 17-32) being that we are now a new man created according to, or "after the likeness of God in true righteousness and holiness (v. 24)." True righteousness and holiness, then, demands that our speech is to be free from corruption. Corrupt words, or evil speaking (v. 31; see 5:4), is not to be found in us since we have put off the old man that was corrupt (v. 22).

In putting on the new man, we have a responsibility to speak in a way that is both edifying and grace imparting. Put differently, our obligation is to build others up in a graceful way. I can think of no better way to truly build others up than through the preaching of the gospel. While your vocational calling might not be to pastor a

Journal:

_____

_____

_____

_____

_____

_____

_____

_____

_____

_____

_____

_____

_____

_____

_____

_____

_____

_____

_____

_____

_____

_____

_____

_____

_____

_____

_____

_____

church, your calling as a Christian is to fulfill the Great Commission, which cannot be accomplished without the preaching of the gospel. In fact, Ephesians 4 teaches us that God has given pastors to equip the saints for the work of ministry and building up of the body of Christ (v. 11-22). Paul, writing in 2 Corinthians 5:20, says, "we are ambassadors for Christ." This is a helpful analogy, since the job of an ambassador is to represent their country in such a way that reflects the values of that particular nation. As ambassadors for Christ, and citizens of the celestial city, we are to represent the values of Christ. This cannot be done through corrupt words; only through the gospel can others truly be built up in grace.

Author and Pastor Tim Keller has stated, "The gospel says you are more sinful and flawed than you ever dared believe, but more accepted and loved than you ever dared hope." This poetic summation of the gospel is both edifying and saturated with grace. Our mission should be to proclaim this message. This will require us to be intentional in how we use our words, since sharing the gospel is never an accident. With this in mind, let us pray for God to create opportunities for us to share the gospel with our family, friends, co-workers, and acquaintances. As Christians called to missional living, this must always be our prayer and focus, lest our failure to make disciples becomes the Great Omission. Pray also that God would help us to be conscientious of our speech so that our communication matches our testimony.

Salt and Light: Ask yourself if your speech truly builds others up in grace. Seek to be a faithful ambassador by living a life with the mission of preaching the gospel with your words.

One Last Thought: Missional living is intentional living. We must be conscientious of what proceeds from our mouth.

Day 10:

Preaching the Gospel: Through Our Worship

Colossians 3:16, "Let the word of Christ dwell in you richly in all wisdom, teaching and admonishing one another in psalms and hymns and spiritual songs, singing with grace in your hearts to the Lord."

As a young boy, I (Christopher) knew that there was something special about my grandmother. I couldn't quite tell what it was for a long time, but I finally realized that what made her different than most of the rest of my family was that she was a Christian. She had given her life to Jesus and was continuously following and worshiping Him. Growing up around her and seeing her model Christ for me, made me want to be like her. It made me want whatever it was that she had. Perhaps you've known someone like that. Maybe it has been someone who lived so differently and had such a different attitude about life that you had to know more about them. Maybe before you became a Christian you had those models in your life as well. One thing is sure for Christians today and that is that we must preach the gospel through our worship. Our worship might be musical in nature, but worship is much more than just music. We must be those models of Christ for others.

The reason that I saw Christ through my grandmother was that she was doing all that she did in the name of Jesus, regardless of the situation that she was in. There were aspects of my family life when I was young that were heartbreaking, but my grandmother worshipped God anyway. There were things that were depressing, but my grandmother was filled with joy. There were times in which much seemed hopeless, but my grandmother had a peace that was beyond understanding. I am reminded of Paul and Silas in the book of Acts. They had their clothes ripped off by an angry mob; the

Journal:

magistrate ordered that they be beaten with rods. They were thrown into the most inner and secure part of a cold, dark, damp prison and placed in the stocks. It seemed as though all hope was lost. After the day that they'd had and whatever was still to come it would make perfect sense if they had given up, laid down in the filth and wept. But it says at midnight they began to sing hymns (cf. Acts 16:22-25). Here Paul and Silas, after enduring such pain, were praising God.

As we make our way through this often-difficult life, we must continue to worship. We must understand that God is in control, that God is good and that God is for us. This type of worship in the midst of pain and turmoil is one of the greatest witnesses that our faith has. The Philippian jailer asked Paul and Silas "Sirs, what must I do to be saved?" I asked the same question of my grandmother. Through your continual worship, others will ask the same of you.

SALT & LIGHT: God help me to worship You in a way in which You are magnified. Help me to show others the reason for the hope that is within me. When the difficulty comes, please use it for Your kingdom's increase.

ONE LAST THOUGHT: Your worship, especially through the difficult times of life, will be a powerful witness for Christ.

Day 11:
Preaching the Gospel: Through Our Actions

James 1:21-26, "Therefore lay aside all filthiness and overflow of wickedness, and receive with meekness the implanted word, which is able to save your souls. But be doers of the word, and not hearers only, deceiving yourselves. For if anyone is a hearer of the word and not a doer, he is like a man observing his natural face in a mirror; for he observes himself, goes away, and immediately forgets what kind of man he was. But he who looks into the perfect law of liberty and continues in it, and is not a forgetful hearer but a doer of the work, this one will be blessed in what he does. If anyone among you things he is religious, and does not bridle his tongue but deceives his own heart, this one's religion is useless."

Jesus could be found reproving sin throughout His ministry on earth. Many times His approach could be interpreted as delicate. However, the same cannot be said whenever He called out the actions of the Pharisees. Nothing seemed to draw out the righteous indignation of Christ quite like the hypocritical lifestyles of the religious elite of His day.

All of us have likely heard the adage, "actions speak louder than words." Jesus was able to see through to the truth of the Pharisees' ministry by viewing their actions. No matter what came out of their mouths, He could see by their actions, or lack thereof, that they only feigned love for God and others. Their hearts had become wicked and selfish and their ministries only pushed people further away from God (cf. Matt. 23:15).

There are many Scripture passages that shed light on God's desire for His people to not only "talk the talk" of a Christian but to more importantly "walk the walk" of one. We must realize that one of the most influential ways we preach the gospel is through our actions.

It has taken many years for me to understand the meaning of James 1:23-24. The Holy Spirit eventually revealed what a crazy, unheard of thing it is for a person to see their image in a

Journal:

_____

_____

_____

_____

_____

_____

_____

_____

_____

_____

_____

_____

_____

_____

_____

_____

_____

_____

_____

_____

mirror and immediately forget what they look like. That should not even be possible! Nor should it be possible for a man or woman to look at their spiritual image through the mirror of Scripture and forget what they see.

Although being an effective witness for Christ involves the use of words too, actions bring to life the words we believe. If our lives do not reflect the message our words preach, witnesses are left to wonder about our true devotion.

God calls us to lives of holiness. Not because our own holiness will bring about salvation but rather because salvation brings about the desire of obedience. That includes obedience to live a holy life that honors God. We are called to be a people who set themselves apart from the sins of this world and who preach a message of good news through our actions.

SALT & LIGHT: God help my actions to be a true reflection of the life You have called me to. Help me to be an effective witness for You through the actions I display to those around me.

ONE LAST THOUGHT: Although being an effective witness for Christ involves the use of words too, actions bring to life the words we believe.

Day 12:

Preaching the Gospel: Through Our Testimony

1 Peter 3:15, "But sanctify the Lord God in your hearts, and always be ready to give a defense to everyone who asks you a reason for the hope that is in you, with meekness and fear."

Imagine the incarnation of Christ: God Himself coming to earth in the likeness of man. Christ came into this world and lived a sinless life!

When we read about the life and testimony of Jesus Christ, we see that He took every crisis and turned it into a way to minister to the needs of others. Whether Jesus was met with a sword, stones, or angry mob; He managed to take each opportunity to demonstrate the gospel.

Perhaps the most peculiar of all is Jesus' death. A seemingly hopeless situation that resulted in the crucifixion of the Messiah was turned into the greatest victory of all time at the will of the Father. Jesus fully understood His missional purpose and the outcome of His time on earth would result in His execution, yet He willingly laid down His life. Unlike Christ, we are uncertain of what each day will bring; but because of how Jesus lived His life we know that when we face opposition that we should use those moments to minister to others.

When Jesus is the Lord of our lives, each crisis becomes an opportunity to witness. We should be ready to give an answer for the hope that is in us. The Greek word that is translated in this passage as "defense" is the word "apologia" from which we get the word apology. However, the idea is not to apologize for the gospel, but to offer a "defense." As Christians, we should always be ready to offer a reason for our hope in Jesus Christ. Even in situations that seem hopeless.

Journal:

As believers, when we live a life full of hope and faith, non-believers will take notice. Non-believers are like an inexperienced running back trying to score a touchdown, but constantly getting tackled. They seemingly have no hope of ever reaching the end zone. As believers, we are called to be missional coaches that help non-believers reach the end zone through Christ. They are more likely to listen to a coach that is speaking from experience. No one wants to take advice from someone who has never played the game or worse... never scored.

Our experience as Christians and our response are a testimony to provide hope to the hopeless.

SALT & LIGHT: Are you ready to defend your reasoning for the hope you have in Jesus Christ?

ONE LAST THOUGHT: Jesus is our example to show us how to be bold in our walk with God, even when times are hard. Our goal should always be to remain in the will of God.

Day 13:

Preaching the Gospel: Through Our Gifts

1 Peter 4:10-11, "As each one has received a gift, minister it to one another, as good stewards of the manifold grace of God. If anyone speaks, let him speak as the oracles of God. If anyone ministers, let him do it as with the ability which God supplies, that in all things God may be glorified through Jesus Christ, to whom belong the glory and the dominion forever and ever. Amen."

Peter tells us that our gifts (spiritual skills given to us by the Holy Spirit) and talents (natural abilities and skills we develop over time) are given to us in order to serve one another and, as a result, bring glory to God. This is one of the primary ways that we, as members of the body, help the church to function as it should. As such, using our gifts is a means of preaching the gospel both corporately and individually.

Corporately by using our gifts to help the church work efficiently and successfully through weekly services. As we use our gifts, whatever they may be, to serve in the church we help to create the opportunity each week for others to hear about Christ. There is simply too much work for only a few people to accomplish on their own. Therefore, we are to use our giftings to do our own share of the work. The more we can take off the plate of our leaders, the more effective we can make their efforts. By helping people find their class, by helping with serving breakfast, by cleaning up messes, or by singing on the praise team, we free up our pastors to focus on the things only they can do.

"For as in one body we have many members, and the members do not all have the same function, so we, though many, are one body in Christ, and individually members one of another. Having gifts that differ according to the grace given to us, let us use them: if prophecy, in proportion to our faith; if service, in our serving; the one who teaches, in his

Journal:

_____

_____

_____

_____

_____

_____

_____

_____

_____

_____

_____

_____

_____

_____

_____

_____

_____

_____

_____

_____

_____

_____

_____

_____

_____

teaching; the one who exhorts, in his exhortation; the one who contributes, in generosity; the one who leads, with zeal; the one who does acts of mercy, with cheerfulness" (Romans 12:4-8 ESV).

By using our gifts we are directly helping the church to fulfill its mission by growing the Body of Christ. "Rather, speaking the truth in love, we are to grow up in every way into him who is the head, into Christ, from whom the whole body, joined and held together by every joint with which it is equipped, when each part is working properly, makes the body grow so that it builds itself up in love" (Ephesians 4:15-16 ESV).

Therefore, this means that every gift, no matter how insignificant it may seem to us is important to the health and growth of the church. Individually we preach the gospel through our gifts and talents, whatever they may be, by creating opportunities to share the gospel. Since no two people are the same, the more ways we can create as a church to reach people the better: some people respond to well reasoned words presented with love and understanding; some respond when we spend time with them as they face difficult times in their life; some respond when we show interest in the same things that they do. This is why the church needs so many different on-ramps for people to get involved and why everything we do should contain the gospel message. We never know what may be that final trigger that helps them accept Jesus as their Savior.

SALT & LIGHT: Ask God to show you where you can use your gifts to serve the church and those around you so that the gospel may be preached effectively.

ONE LAST THOUGHT: A sign of missional living and spiritual maturity is when we take off the bib and put on the apron!

Day 14:
Preaching the Gospel: The Mount Vision
Mark 16:15, "Go into all the world and preach the gospel to every creature."

This week we have examined the method of the Great Commission, "to preach the gospel." We often think of preaching as the task of the preacher. However, the command to "preach the gospel to every creature" is the task of every disciple. Together we are preaching a cosmic sermon with our words, worship, actions, testimony, and gifts. The Apostle Paul explains that the church should understand and make known the gospel and even "principalities and powers in the heavenly places" are paying attention to our cosmic sermon (cf. Eph. 3:10).

The preaching of God's Word should promote life-change that produces Christ-likeness. This is true not only for the sermon that is delivered from the pulpit, but the sermon that is delivered from your life.

Our culture has a narrative that says, "It's my life and I'll do what I want." However, this is not the motto of the authentic Christ-following disciple. Apparently this attitude was the same in Paul's day, "'I have the right to do anything,' you say – but not everything is beneficial" (1 Cor. 6:12). Paul's words ring true today, you may have the right to do as you please, "but not everything is beneficial." In other words, if it does not produce Christ-likeness it is not constructive.

There are some basic principles in preparing a sermon. These same principles are true for the authentic Christ-following disciple who is committed to missional living.

First, God's Word is the starting point. God's Word should be the authority for our life.

Journal:

When we seek to discern the right path for life's choices, our greatest concern is not the advice of others but the Word of God. The Christian who lives life without first opening the Word of God each day is like the folly of a preacher who attempts to preach without having opened his Bible.

Second, the gospel should be the focus of our living. If the gospel is central to our preaching, the gospel is central to our living. Our lives should be marked with redemption through the grace of God. Others will see our faults, fears, failures, and frustrations and yet they should observe the grace of God that produces Christ-likeness. When our lives are consumed with the missional living of the gospel, we are not the central focus... Christ is!

Third, the call to respond is one of worship. "Let your light so shine before men, that they may see your good works and glorify your Father in heaven" (Matt. 5:16). My desire is to preach the inspired Word of God with such faithfulness and sensitivity that God's voice will be heard and His people obey Him. The same should be true of missional living. We should desire to be so faithful to the Word of God that people do not focus on us, but rather focus on bringing glory to our heavenly Father.

SALT & LIGHT: Lord, may the lives we live preach the sermon You desire. May we begin each day with Your Word, may we live out the gospel, and may our actions bring glory and honor to Your name. Amen.

ONE LAST THOUGHT: Missional living is like preaching a sermon each and every day.

Small Group Guide for Week 2: **The Method**

SMALL GROUP APPRENTICE

WELCOME: If you have new members, take time to briefly introduce yourselves.

PRAYER: Take some time to pray for your group before you begin the lesson.

SPIRITUAL HABITS: Take some time to review the Spiritual HABITS. Ask how the group is doing keeping up with the daily devotions (this is the "H" in HABITS). Ask if anyone needs Scripture Memory Key Tags (this is the "B" in HABITS).

TOPIC TEASER: "Spiritual Gifts Inventory"
How do spiritual gifts help us fulfill the Great Commission? Consider sharing your spiritual gifts and encouraging one another in using those gifts! (See Appendix C on page 171)

READ THE SCRIPTURES:
Ask for a volunteer in the group to read Mark 16:15-16. Consider reading it a few times from different translations.

STUDY THE SCRIPTURES:
What is the *method* of the Great Commission?

DISCUSSION:
Use the space below to take notes on your discussion of the devotions.

_____
_____
_____
_____
_____
_____
_____
_____
_____
_____
_____
_____
_____
_____
_____
_____
_____
_____
_____
_____

APPLY THE SCRIPTURES:

A passage of Scripture has a specific meaning, but has many points of application. As a group, discuss how you have been challenged to live missionally as a result of your time in God's Word this week?

MY PERSONAL ACTION STEP:

What do you think God wants you to do as a result of your studies and small group discussion this week?

_____

_____

_____

MISSIONS PROJECT:

As a group make a final decision concerning your mission project. Write down some key details here:

_____

_____

_____

_____

_____

_____

_____

SNEAK PEEK:

Next week we will focus on the *message* of the Great Commission.

PRAYER REQUESTS & PRAYER:

Take prayer requests and close in prayer.

_____

_____

_____

_____

_____

_____

_____

_____

_____

LEADER NOTE:

Dismiss your group, but make yourself available to anyone who has questions.

Week 3

Luke: The Message

This week we will focus on Luke's account of the Great Commission and the message for making disciples. That message is nothing less than the gospel.

"And He opened their understanding, that they might comprehend the Scriptures. Then He said to them, 'Thus it is written, and thus it was necessary for the Christ to suffer and to rise from the dead the third day, and that repentance and remission of sins should be preached in His name to all nations, beginning at Jerusalem. And you are witnesses of these things. Behold, I send the Promise of My Father upon you; but tarry in the city of Jerusalem until you are endued with power from on high.'"
Luke 24:45-49

Day 15:

The Good News

Luke 24:45-49, "And He opened their understanding, that they might comprehend the Scriptures. Then He said to them, 'Thus it is written, and thus it was necessary for the Christ to suffer and to rise from the dead the third day, and that repentance and remission of sins should be preached in His name to all nations, beginning at Jerusalem. And you are witnesses of these things. Behold, I send the Promise of My Father upon you; but tarry in the city of Jerusalem until you are endued with power from on high.'"

Luke sums up all the history of Israel, Jesus' life, and the future of the church in his account of the Great Commission, making the emphasis the message itself: the gospel. It is important to remember that the gospel is not just the narrative of Jesus' life, but also the entirety of the divine plan of redemption from beginning to end, from creation to restoration. As such, the fulfillment of prophecy is important to the message we deliver, for it tells us what the necessary elements are and that they were always God's plan: that Christ was to suffer, that He would rise from the dead, and that repentance and remission of sins are to be proclaimed to the nations.

From the very beginning it was God's plan to send the Son to suffer and die upon the cross to restore the relationship with man, "And I will put enmity between you and the woman, and between your seed and her seed; He shall bruise your head, and you shall bruise His heel." (Gen. 3:15b). Two of the clearest foretellings of this are found in Isaiah 53 and Psalm 22. Blood is necessary for the forgiveness of sin (cf. Lev. 17:11; Heb. 9:22). While the human participants, and Satan, thought they were running the show during Jesus' death, God was in complete control and simply fulfilling His promise to deliver us.

The prophecies of the resurrection are more subtle. However, Isaiah 53 does have hints of the resurrection. After the Servant suffers for

Journal:

our sins and is "cut off out of the land of the living," Isaiah states that He will "see His seed" and that God will "prolong His days"(cf. 53:10), implying that He is again alive as well. The clearest reference, however, is found in Psalm 16:10, "For Thou wilt not abandon my soul to Sheol; neither wilt Thou allow Thy Holy One to undergo decay." In order to not decay, death could not be a lasting condition. Christ's resurrection guarantees our own at His second coming by demonstrating His divinity and power over death (cf. Eph. 2:6).

Of all the prophecies about Christ in the Old Testament, especially important to Luke is Isaiah 49:6: "Indeed He says, 'It is too small a thing that You should be My Servant to raise up the tribes of Jacob, and to restore the preserved ones of Israel; I will also give You as a light to the Gentiles, that You should be My salvation to the ends of the earth.'"

This verse is one of the most important emphases in both Luke and Acts. When Simeon blesses Jesus at the temple he references this passage (cf. Luke 2:32). Luke hints at it in his second-volume account of the Great Commission found in Acts 1:8. Paul uses it in his reasoning for turning to the Gentiles at Psidian Antioch (cf. Acts 13:47). From the very beginning, the prophecies concerning Christ contained the audience of His message: the whole world. Salvation was never intended for Israel alone. The Messiah was not sent to earth to restore the kingdom of Israel but to be God's "salvation to the ends of the earth."

SALT & LIGHT: Can you identify and share the four themes of the gospel (i.e. creation, fall, redemption, and restoration)?

ONE LAST THOUGHT: The gospel is the message of the Great Commission.

Day 16:

The Good News: The Suffering of Christ

1 Peter 3:18, "For Christ also suffered once for sins, the just for the unjust, that He might bring us to God, being put to death in the flesh but made alive by the Spirit."

The most bittersweet event that the world has ever known was the suffering of Christ on the cross. The perfect and spotless name was despised and rejected. He was beaten, mocked, and spat upon. He was paraded through the streets, carrying a cross while many glared and heckled. His hands and feet were nailed to the beams of the cross and it was raised for all to see. This event is bitter because we all know that if anyone ever deserved to be treated this way, it wasn't Jesus. He was perfect, yet He was punished. He was sinless; yet slain. He had committed no crime, yet He was crucified. Christ's suffering was sweet because through it, we can be brought to God. The chasm that had lain between God and humans had been forever bridged. Christ's suffering and death are our only source for life, and more abundant life than we could have ever imagined.

It seems almost insane to imagine that Christ's suffering and death could be considered Good News, but it is the very best news that hopeless sinners could receive. Consider anew Isaiah 53:5 when the prophet writes, "But he was pierced for our transgressions, he was crushed for our iniquities; the punishment that brought us peace was on him, and by his wounds we are healed." The healing of our souls is made possible by the injuries, which Jesus sustained. Our hope of eternal life is only found in the death of our Lord. One of my favorite lines from any hymn that has ever been written speaks of the beauty of the bittersweet suffering of Christ. Perhaps you remember it as well.

Journal:

_____
_____
_____
_____
_____
_____
_____
_____
_____
_____
_____
_____
_____
_____
_____
_____
_____
_____
_____
_____
_____
_____
_____
_____
_____
_____
_____
_____
_____
_____
_____
_____

My sin, oh, the bliss of this glorious thought!
My sin, not in part but the whole,
Is nailed to the cross, and I bear it no more,
Praise the Lord, praise the Lord, O my soul!

Through the cross and the suffering of Christ, the world saw the fullest, clearest, most powerful, and most overwhelming display of the grace and love of God. Through Jesus' suffering and death, God told the world that He loved us. It is incomparably important that we tell the world that Jesus suffered and died for them!

SALT & LIGHT: God help me to share the gospel with people all around me. Let my focus always be on the cross.

ONE LAST THOUGHT: The world must know the gospel. A gospel that fails to mention all that Jesus endured for the sake of lost sinners is not *the* gospel.

Day 17:

The Good News: Raising to Life

1 Corinthians 15:13-14, "But if there is no resurrection of the dead, then Christ is not risen. And if Christ is not risen, then our preaching is empty and your faith is also empty."

There are only two options when it comes to the resurrection of Jesus Christ: Either Jesus was resurrected, or He wasn't. Paul gives detail in 1 Corinthians 15:12-20 on why the resurrection of Jesus Christ it essential to the Christian faith. Paul is pleading that if Christ had not been resurrected, then nobody else would be either. That would then mean that Christianity was a lie and that our preaching of the gospel would be in vain. If that were true, then ultimately people would have no hope. Eternal life would mean absolutely nothing. Paul makes it clear that Jesus has indeed been raised from the dead. Paul was one of the greatest witnesses if the resurrection. As an unbeliever he was convinced that Jesus was dead. The radical change in his own life was evidence that Jesus had been raised from the dead. At this point if you were with Paul or simply reading this passage then you would probably say, "Yes, I agree that Jesus raised form the dead." Then if you believe that then you should believe in the resurrection of all the dead. Simply known that Christ came as a man, truly human and experienced all that we experience and still lived a sinless life. If this never happened and if Christ never rose from the dead then there is no gospel to preach.

Paul continues to explain the truth behind this in verses 1st Corinthians 22-28. Adam's sin had separated mankind from God, but Jesus' sacrifice redeemed them all and restored an intimate relationship. The resurrection of Jesus is God's ultimate victory over sin and death. Those of us who call Jesus as our Lord and Savior will live on for an eternity with Christ, but

Journal:

_____
_____
_____
_____
_____
_____
_____
_____
_____
_____
_____
_____
_____
_____
_____
_____
_____
_____
_____
_____
_____
_____
_____
_____
_____
_____
_____
_____
_____

those who turn their backs on Him will spend eternity in hell, separated from God.

If this story of Jesus is true then life is beautiful, life is glorious, and we have eternity to look forward to with Him if we have a relationship with Him. If this story turns out to be a mystery, then it becomes a riddle that has left us with blankness and blackness of eternal despair. The Bible and historic evidence shows us that this story is true. Christ was, Christ is, and He was a living person. He is with His people, guiding and protecting us, but also leading us to the day of our own glorious resurrection.

Think about it this way, the disciples knew the resurrection of Christ to be a fact. A fact they believed with such certainty that they were willing to die for it. They shared the gospel with such compassion and faced many trials as a result of their sharing, but they never once denied the resurrection of Christ.

SALT & LIGHT: Father in Heaven; thank you for sending your Son to die on the cross for my sins, my failures, and my wrongdoings. I know that I will continue to fail, but through your Son I have forgiveness. Thank you Jesus for defeating the grave and conquering death so that I may have life and have it abundantly. Thank you for the promise of eternity. Amen

ONE LAST THOUGHT: Everything that we believe in as believers rests on the resurrection of Jesus Christ.

Day 18:

The Good News: Repentance & Remission of Sins

Luke 24:45-49, "And He opened their understanding, that they might comprehend the Scriptures. Then He said to them, 'Thus it is written, and thus it was necessary for the Christ to suffer and to rise from the dead the third day, and that <u>repentance and remission of sins</u> should be preached in His name to all nations, beginning at Jerusalem. And you are witnesses of these things. Behold, I send the Promise of My Father upon you; but tarry in the city of Jerusalem until you are endued with power from on high.'"

Have you ever broken your mother's lamp from playing a blindfold game in the living room? Have you ever broken a neighbor's window from throwing baseball? Have you ever been playing basketball and the ball shatters the kitchen window? Have you ever been hired to mow your neighbor's yard and unwittingly mowed down their flowers? Have you ever pranked your neighbors by ordering pizza delivery to their house only to get caught because you were watching and laughing from your own front porch? I (Chris) have done all of these and the list could continue with the countless things I have done that needed forgiveness.

The word "remission" means "forgiveness." The word "repentance" means "to change your mind." Luke's usage of these two words together laid the foundation for the third theme of the gospel: redemption. If it were written out as a math problem, it would look like this...

repentance + remission = redemption

When we "change our mind" and decide that God's way is better than our way, then our actions will change as well. At the same time, God forgives us. This powerful combination of repentance through faith and the remission of sins are essential to the gospel narrative.

Journal:

_____
_____
_____
_____
_____
_____
_____
_____
_____
_____
_____
_____
_____
_____
_____
_____
_____
_____
_____
_____
_____
_____
_____

Notice the basis for this forgiveness is not found in us, but in the death, burial, and resurrection of Christ. Luke 24:46, "Then He (Jesus) said to them, 'Thus it is written, and thus it was necessary for the Christ to suffer and to rise from the dead the third day." Paul explains this same truth, "being justified freely by His grace through the redemption that is in Christ Jesus, whom God set forth as a propitiation by His blood, through faith, to demonstrate His righteousness, because in His forbearance God had passed over the sins that were previously committed" (Romans 3:24-25).

SALT & LIGHT: Have you experienced the redemption of Christ that comes through repentance and remission of sins? If not, take a moment to read "How to Become a Christian" on page 151.

ONE LAST THOUGHT: By grace through faith in the resurrected Christ we experience redemption!

Day 19:
The Good News: Adoption as Sons

Romans 8:14-17, "For as many as are led by the Spirit, these are the sons of God. For you did not receive the spirit of bondage again to fear, but you received the Spirit of adoption by whom we cry out, 'Abba, Father.' The Spirit Himself bears witness with our spirit that we are children of God, and if children, then heirs-heirs of God and joint heirs with Christ, if indeed we suffer with Him, that we may also be glorified together."

Galatians 4:4-5, "But when the fullness of time had come, God sent for His Son, born of a woman, born under the law to redeem those who were under the law, that we might receive the adoption as sons."

There are many reasons why the message of Jesus Christ is good news. One of the greatest is that through the redemptive blood of Jesus, we can be adopted as children of God! Imagine that, we can call the Creator of the Universe our daddy!

The Latin phrase "quid pro quo" means something for something. It is a phrase often used in the legal or business world to imply if you do something for me, I'll do something for you. But the good news of Romans 8 and Galatians 4 is that the benefit of adoption is free for the taking. Becoming a child of God through adoption is free of charge. It could be said that it is "quid pro nihilio", meaning something for nothing!

Part of the Good News of salvation is that once we open the free gift of God's salvation by accepting His son Jesus, we have become a joint heir with Jesus. That means Christ is our brother, we are a child to God and we are recipients of the Holy Spirit.

Many people who have been adopted will tell you that initially it was hard to believe that someone would love them and accept them without reason. They have trouble accepting that level of love after being rejected. Once they truly embrace the fact that they are

Journal:

_____

_____

_____

_____

_____

_____

_____

_____

_____

_____

_____

_____

_____

_____

_____

_____

_____

_____

_____

_____

_____

loved and accepted through no merit of their own, it brings a feeling of peace and favor that the world could never possibly provide.

Paul uses examples in Romans and Galatians of how God has adopted believers into His family, no strings attached. We no longer have to be ashamed or hurt over the rejection of the world. We can rejoice in knowing that the free gift of adoption and all the benefits that go along with it are ours to enjoy through accepting His son.

Something for nothing... now that is Good News!

SALT & LIGHT: Abba, Father, thank You for adopting me into Your family. Thank You for Jesus, a friend that sticks closer than a brother. May You strengthen my resolve to tell others how they can receive adoption as sons through Jesus.

ONE LAST THOUGHT: Becoming a child of God through adoption is free of charge.

Day 20:
The Good News: Lost in Translation

Luke 24:45-49, "And He opened their understanding, that they might comprehend the Scriptures. Then He said to them, 'Thus it is written, and thus it was necessary for the Christ to suffer and to rise from the dead the third day, and that repentance and remission of sins should be preached in His name to all nations, beginning at Jerusalem. And you are witnesses of these things. Behold, I send the Promise of My Father upon you; but tarry in the city of Jerusalem until you are endued with power from on high.'"

At the beginning of the Great Commission in Luke, we are told that Jesus opened the understanding of the disciples to comprehend His message. Until this time, it was as if Jesus had been speaking another language to the disciples (cf. Luke 2:50; 9:45). What seems obvious to us was completely lost upon those who were listening to Jesus. This is because we have a spiritual understanding through the Holy Spirit they did not. However, the world today, like the early disciples, does not have this spiritual sight either. It is necessary for us to translate God's message through our lives (i.e. our words and actions) to help other people understand what God wants to tell them.

The core of the message we are to deliver is that of repentance and forgiveness. However, instead of being bearers of the good news of the gospel, Christians are frequently barriers of hate and judgment. Take a moment and think about how the world thinks about the church today. Do they think of the church as a place of love and forgiveness? Or is it a place of hatred and judgment? The real message of the gospel is getting lost in translation. When someone shares the gospel, the conduct and character of the messenger cannot be separated from the message. Because we are sharing a set of values and morals as part of the message our own actions and attitudes reflect upon the gospel. Therefore, our actions have direct consequences upon its reception. In everything we do we should seek to see

Journal:

people and do things as Jesus did. This goes beyond just morality. When Jesus came to earth, He became one with those He was sent to serve. He lived among them and shared in their weakness and struggles. As such, we should also become one with those whom we are sent to help. We cannot truly take the gospel to others successfully if we do not share in their lives in the same way.

Some years ago Peter K. Haile, assistant headmaster of the Stony Brook School on Long Island, told a story that illustrates this point and gives a closing challenge. He had a missionary friend, a woman doctor, who went to India on rather short notice because of a pressing need in a certain hospital. She had not had time to go to language school but instead was put to work in the hospital immediately, where she spoke through an interpreter. After she had been there a while she wrote to the Hailes expressing frustration and discouragement. She had been trying to show love and gentleness to the people, but they did not seem to be responding. She asked them to pray about it. A few weeks later another letter came, this time saying that she had discovered what they problem was. It was the translator. She had been loving, but he was apparently a rude, arrogant fellow who never conveyed her concern for the patients at all. He was a barrier to her message. (Boice, The Gospel of John, vol. 5, 1598).

The account above shows us why we must be careful about what message we are sending. Are we more concerned about pointing out the sins of others making them feel judged and hated? Or are we known for our message of God's forgiveness and redemption? The souls of those we may help in leading to Christ through our words and actions are forever. We can either help lead them to Christ or spur them on their way to Hell.

SALT & LIGHT: What picture of Jesus do others have through your actions and words? Are you communicating the love of Christ?

ONE LAST THOUGHT: The life you live in front of non-believers is like a translation guide to help others understand the gospel.

Day 21:

The Good News: The Mount Vision

Luke 24:45-49, "And He opened their understanding, that they might comprehend the Scriptures. Then He said to them, 'Thus it is written, and thus it was necessary for the Christ to suffer and to rise from the dead the third day, and that repentance and remission of sins should be preached in His name to all nations, beginning at Jerusalem. And you are witnesses of these things. Behold, I send the Promise of My Father upon you; but tarry in the city of Jerusalem until you are endued with power from on high."

Journal:

This week we have examined the message of the Great Commission, "the gospel." The Bible does not have separate gospels for different people, age groups, or cultures. The message is for all kinds of people and begins with the Jews (cf. Acts 2:5-11) and then for the Gentiles (cf. Acts 13:46; Romans 1:16). The message of the Great Commission is the gospel and has been God's plan since before the foundation of the world (cf. 1 Peter 1:20). God is never caught by surprise. God knew before He created mankind that we would sin and had already made His plan for redemption and restoration through Christ!

CREATION: The message of the Great Commission is that God created you and loves you. You were created to enjoy a personal relationship with God. Even before God created the foundation of the earth, you were the focus of His love.

"Blessed by the God and Father of our Lord Jesus Christ, who has blessed us with every spiritual blessing in the heavenly places in Christ, just as He chose us in Him before the foundation of the world, that we should be holy and without blame before Him in love" (Ephesians 1:3-4).

THE FALL: That special relationship with God was broken because of sin. Sin separates us from God and causes us to live our lives outside of His will.

"All we like sheep have gone astray; we have turned, every one, to his own way" (Is 53:6).

"If we say that we have no sin, we deceive ourselves, and the truth is not in us" (1 Jn 1:8).

"But your iniquities (sins) have separated you from you God" (Isaiah 59:2).

"For all have sinned and fall short of the glory of God" (Romans 3:23).

REDEMPTION: God came to earth as a human being (i.e. Jesus) to bring us back to Himself. We need forgiveness of our sin in order to have a relationship with God. Jesus died on the cross to pay your penalty for sin. He did this so we can have a relationship with Him again.

"Jesus said, 'I am the way, the truth, and the life. No one comes to the Father except through Me'" (John 14:6).

"For the wages of sin is death, but the gift of God is eternal life in Christ Jesus our Lord" (Romans 6:23).

"But God demonstrates His own love toward us, in that while we were still sinners, Christ died for us" (Romans 5:8).

RESTORATION: When you accept Christ as your Savior, the Holy Spirit works within you to make you more Christ-like in character. You will continue to sin and make mistakes, but the Holy Spirit works within you to help you grow in spiritual maturity. One day you will be fully restored and get to meet Christ face-to-face and spend eternity with Him in heaven. Those who never accept Christ will continue to be separated from God into eternity.

"that you put off, concerning your former conduct, the old man which grows corrupt according to the deceitful lusts, and be renewed in the spirit of your mind, and that you put on the new man which was created according to God, in true righteousness and holiness" (Ephesians 4:22-24).

"But as He who called you is holy, you also be holy in all your conduct" (1 Peter 1:15).

"For now we see in a mirror, dimly, but then face to face. Now I know in part, but then I shall know just as I also am known" (1 Corinthians 13:12).

As you can see, the message of the Great Commission is not just "how to be saved;" the gospel is God's continuing work in your life even after you are saved! Therefore, sharing the gospel is not a single event, but something we are called to do every single day. That's missional living!

SALT & LIGHT: Dear Jesus, thank You for creating me and loving me, even when I've ignored You and gone my own way. I realize I need You in my life and I'm sorry for my sins. I ask You to forgive me. Thank You for dying on the cross for me. Please help me to understand it more. As much as I know how, I want to follow You from now on. Please come into my life and make me a new person inside. I accept Your gift of salvation. Please help me to grow now as a Christian. Amen.

ONE LAST THOUGHT: Missional living is about the message of the gospel being proclaimed in my daily life.

Small Group Guide for Week 3: **The Message**

WELCOME: If you have new members, take time to briefly introduce yourselves.

PRAYER: Take some time to pray for your group before your begin the lesson.

SPIRITUAL HABITS: Take some time to review the Spiritual HABITS. Ask how the group is doing keeping up with the daily devotions (this is the "H" in HABITS). Ask if anyone needs Scripture Memory Key Tags (this is the "B" in HABITS).

TOPIC TEASER: "Sharing the Gospel"
Have you ever shared the gospel with someone? What were the circumstances? How did it go? What would it take for you to share the gospel with someone this week?

READ THE SCRIPTURES:
Ask for a volunteer in the group to read Luke 24:45-49. Consider reading it a few times from different translations.

STUDY THE SCRIPTURES:
What is the *message* of the Great Commission?

DISCUSSION:
Use the space below to take notes on your discussion of the devotions.

_____
_____
_____
_____
_____
_____
_____
_____
_____
_____
_____
_____
_____
_____
_____
_____
_____
_____
_____

APPLY THE SCRIPTURES:

A passage of Scripture has a specific meaning, but has many points of application. As a group, discuss how you have been challenged to live missionally as a result of your time in God's Word this week?

PERSONAL

MY PERSONAL ACTION STEP:

What do you think God wants you to do as a result of your studies and small group discussion this week?

_____
_____
_____

MISSIONS COORDINATOR

MISSIONS PROJECT:

Ask your Small Group Missions Coordinator to give an update. Write down some key details here:

_____
_____
_____
_____
_____
_____

SNEAK PEEK:

Next week we will focus on the *authority* of the Great Commission.

PRAYER REQUESTS & PRAYER:

Take prayer requests and close in prayer.

_____
_____
_____
_____
_____
_____
_____
_____

LEADER NOTE:

Dismiss your group, but make yourself available to anyone who has questions.

Week 4

John: The Authority

This week we will focus on John's account of the Great Commission and the authority for making disciples. God the Father gave all authority to Christ and then Christ commissioned us to carry out His continued mission.

"So Jesus said to them again, 'Peace to you! As the Father has sent Me, I also send you.' And when He had said this, He breathed on them, and said to them, 'Receive the Holy Spirit.'"
John 20:21-22

Day 22:
Being Like Our Master

John 20:21-22, "So Jesus said to them again, 'Peace to you! As the Father has sent Me, I also send you.' And when He had said this, He breathed on them, and said to them, 'Receive the Holy Spirit.'"

John's emphasis in his account of the Great Commission is the authority behind the mission: Christ. In fact, this is the message throughout the Gospel of John. Each of the Gospels paints Jesus in a slightly different light. This can be seen in the genealogies found within the Gospels. Matthew, the most Jewish in orientation, begins Jesus' family history with Abraham the founder of the Hebrew patriarchs. Luke, the most Greek in orientation, takes Christ's family line all the way back to Adam, the root of all men. However, John, takes us back even further; all the way back to the beginning of time showing Jesus as God. It is by, through, and for Him that all things were created and find their meaning.

What is particularly interesting is that even as God, Jesus placed His authority on earth as being from the Father and not Himself. If our master, as God, did this, so must we. In addition to the focus on authority here in John, it can also be found in Matthew's account, "All authority has been given to Me in heaven and on earth. Go therefore" (Matt. 28:18b). A basic rule of exegesis is to "pay attention to 'therefores' because they are *there for* a reason." The therefore in Matthew 28:19 is no exception, and possibly one of the most important of all. Our commission depends, directly, upon the authority that has been given to Jesus. Now, in John 20:21-23, Jesus passes that same authority over to the church through our commission. As such, we can view the church's mission as a continuation of His mission; we exercise Christ's authority by sharing His message as His Body here on earth.

Journal:

God sent Christ to earth for a purpose, a purpose that is ongoing. This is supported by the text. The Greek word for "sent" (i.e., ἀπέσταλκέν, apestalken) is in the perfect tense, indicating an ongoing condition. We are not doing a new work apart from that purpose, but He is continuing His work through us. As we go to the world we exercise Christ's purpose and authority in reaching the world. So what does it look like to carry on the work of Christ in the world? It means being like our master and proclaiming the same message that he was sent to deliver. We can find this purpose in Isaiah:

"The Spirit of the Lord God *is* upon Me,
Because the Lord has anointed Me
To preach good tidings to the poor;
He has sent Me to heal the brokenhearted,
To proclaim liberty to the captives,
And the opening of the prison to *those who are* bound;
To proclaim the acceptable year of the Lord,
And the day of vengeance of our God;
To comfort all who mourn,
To console those who mourn in Zion,
To give them beauty for ashes,
The oil of joy for mourning,
The garment of praise for the spirit of heaviness;
That they may be called trees of righteousness,
The planting of the LORD, that He may be glorified" (Isaiah 61:1-3).

Take careful notice of the list, particularly that it not only lists salvation but practical day-to-day needs as well. He was sent to proclaim good tidings to those who are poor. He was sent to proclaim liberty to the captive. He was sent to comfort the hurting. This is our message through Christ's authority. We are to be about helping those that need help; giving comfort to the hurting; providing liberty to the captive; and ultimately, about giving glory of God.

SALT & LIGHT: Lord, help me to know the gospel better so I can faithfully fulfill what You have entrusted to me.

ONE LAST THOUGHT: Knowing we are exercising Christ's authority when we share the gospel should give us confidence. Remember we are only the messengers and the real work is God's hands. So, be bold!

Day 23:

Being Like Our Master: Filled with the Spirit

Isaiah 61:1a, "The Spirit of the Lord GOD is upon Me, because the LORD has anointed Me to preach good tidings to the poor."

Journal:

_____
_____
_____
_____
_____
_____
_____
_____
_____
_____
_____
_____
_____
_____
_____
_____
_____
_____
_____
_____
_____
_____
_____
_____
_____
_____

I would guess you have been in a church service in which something like this was prayed... "God, please fill this place with Your presence today." It is one of the things that churches pray most for when gathered together, and they should. To be in God's presence is certainly the best place we can be. Now, theologically speaking, God is omnipresent. He is everywhere; always. God can and does allow His presence to be manifested in different ways and intensities, however. That is something that hopefully you've noticed as well. Sometimes it is like a still small voice while you're quiet and alone. Sometimes it is like a consuming fire when you're worshipping together with other believers.

Have you ever noticed how many of God's promises of His abiding presence are interwoven with action and missions? The verse above is only one of many. Through the Scriptures we can see that God's presence is most intense in our lives when we submit to the plans that He has for us. He provides the Holy Spirit because of the mission and it is through the mission itself that we most fully experience God. Take the following as a few more examples...

"Therefore go and make disciples of all nations... and surely I am with you always" (Matthew 28:19-20).

"Whoever serves me must follow me; and where I am, my servant also will be" (John 12:26).

"The Lord replied, 'My Presence will go with you, and I will give you rest'" (Exodus 33:14).

"Then he said to them all: 'Whoever wants to be my disciple must deny themselves and take up their cross daily and follow me'" (Luke 9:23).

"But you shall receive power when the Holy Spirit has come upon you; and you shall be witnesses to me in Jerusalem, and in all Judea and Samaria, and to the ends of the earth" (Acts 1:8).

We see through many biblical examples that "being with Christ" means following Him. It means doing what He does. To follow in the footsteps of Jesus has always been, and will always be, more than following Him to church. It will mean following Him everywhere; even to the very gates of Hell in search of the lost. We also see that the presence of the Holy Spirit is connected to the mission that we were created for. Though the Holy Spirit dwells within all born-again believers, it is most powerfully felt when living out the Great Commission!

One verse of the hymn "Footprints of Jesus" comes to mind.

> *If they lead through the temple holy,*
> *preaching the word;*
> *Or in homes of the poor and lowly,*
> *serving the Lord.*
> *Footsteps of Jesus,*
> *that make the pathway glow;*
> *We will follow the steps of Jesus*
> *where e'er they go.*

The simple words to the hymn carry a profound biblical message. We are called to go. No matter where and no matter what we are called to follow Christ. Another important realization to make is that Jesus we are not simply obeying orders when we go, but we are following the model that Jesus himself lived out. The only hope we have of singing a song with sincerity, like the one above, is found if God's presence is within us. We will never be able to genuinely follow Christ wherever He leads without the indwelling of the Holy Spirit. We need His power and guidance to truly follow Him. Our obedience to the Great Commission will magnify His presence in our lives.

SALT & LIGHT: God help me to not arbitrarily request Your presence for my own sake. Rather, help me to feel Your presence as I live my life for You. I know that the Holy Spirit lives within me, and I ask that You would help me to more fully realize and utilize His power and presence through living missionally.

ONE LAST THOUGHT: God's presence and the Great Commission go hand in hand. God is most powerfully felt and experienced when we truly live our lives on mission for Him.

Day 24:
Being Like Our Master: Bearers of Good Things

Isaiah 61:1b, "To preach good tidings to the poor; He has sent Me to heal the brokenhearted, to proclaim liberty among the captives, and the opening of the prison to those who are bound."

Isaiah 61:1 gives us a prophetic look at the ministry of Jesus and also our own mission as followers of Christ. Since we are called to be like Christ, we must look to His ministry and the things He did. Isaiah 61 gives us that mission, especially when you look to Jesus' ministry. Jesus fulfills this prophecy and speaks of it during His ministry (cf. Luke 4:16-30). Jesus takes the scroll and reads this passage. Once He concludes the reading, He begins to speak and tell us that, "today as you listen, this scripture has been fulfilled." Jesus has fulfilled the prophecy; He has been anointed with the Holy Spirit to preach good news to the poor. He was sent to release the captives and restore sight to the blind. Jesus fulfills this mission that the Lord has given Him. As a result, we have new life. We have a life with Him because of the rich history of Christ followers who have followed in the footsteps of Jesus. They wanted to see good news spread throughout all nations. We are called to do the same as well.

Isaiah identifies in chapter 61 those who need to hear the gospel. He doesn't simply say all people, but instead he gives a description of people: the poor, the brokenhearted, captives and prisoners, and those who mourn. Perhaps we can all identify with this list. We are all poor without Jesus, brokenhearted without Jesus, captives and prisoners to our sin without Jesus. We have all mourned without Jesus. Jesus brought the Good News to each of us through someone else. We heard the good news and responded to it. If we have responded to that message with an affirmation to begin a relationship with Christ,

Journal:

_____
_____
_____
_____
_____
_____
_____
_____
_____
_____
_____
_____
_____
_____
_____
_____
_____
_____
_____
_____
_____
_____
_____
_____
_____
_____
_____
_____

then we are no longer poor for we have the riches of Christ. We are no longer brokenhearted, because Christ lives within us. We are no longer captives and prisoners of sin, but redeemed and forgiven by the blood of Christ. We no longer mourn, but rejoice in Christ! He has come to rescue us.

Many of us have received the good news and responded to it with a relationship with Christ. However, many in our community have yet to respond to the message of Christ and many of them have never even heard that message. If we want to be bearers of good tidings then we must be looking for opportunities to care for those who are hurting without Christ. Think back to your life before you knew Christ and how things changed when He healed you from your brokenness and when He restored you from your sin. We must remember daily that He has saved us from death. In response, our hearts should break for those that do not have a relationship with Christ and we should bring them the good news.

SALT & LIGHT: Jesus, thank You for modeling a life that I strive to follow daily. I know that I miss opportunities to share Your good news. God, break my heart today for those that our hurting without You. Show me one person that is broken today, so that I may share Your good news and comfort them with Your love. Amen.

ONE LAST THOUGHT: We must not become comfortable in our walk with Christ that we forget about those that are broken and without Christ. We have the good news and we need to be bearers of good tidings.

Day 25:

Being Like Our Master: Messengers of Peace

Isaiah 61:2, "To proclaim the acceptable year of the LORD, and the day of vengeance of our God; to comfort all who mourn."

John 20:21-22, "So Jesus said to them again, 'Peace to you! As the Father has sent Me, I also send you.' And when He had said this, He breathed on them, and said to them, 'Receive the Holy Spirit.'"

One of the biggest obstacles to sharing the gospel is fear. As believers we have a number of excuses as to why we do not share the gospel with others, all of which can essentially be reduced to fear of something: a fear of what people will think, a fear of not knowing what to say, a fear of rejection, or a fear of failure to name a few.

The key to overcoming these fears is peace. This is why Jesus begins with "Peace to you" (cf. v. 21). In fact, within eight verses Jesus greets the disciples three times with, "Peace to you" (cf. v. 19, 21, 26). Within the Gospel of John, Jesus tells the disciples that He was sent to give peace on two other occasions outside of chapter 20.

"Peace I leave with you, My peace I give to you; not as the world gives do I give to you. Let not your heart be troubled, neither let it be afraid" (John 14:27).

"These things I have spoken to you, that in Me you may have peace. In the world you will have tribulation; but be of good cheer, I have overcome the world" (John 16:33).

The gospel is a message of peace not fear (cf. Rom. 8:6; 10:15; 14:17). This includes both peace *with* and *of* God. We must possess the peace God gives if we are ever to successfully share the gospel with the world.

Journal:

_____
_____
_____
_____
_____
_____
_____
_____
_____
_____
_____
_____
_____
_____
_____
_____
_____
_____
_____
_____
_____
_____
_____
_____
_____

Peace *with* God

"For He Himself is our peace, who has made both one, and has broken down the middle wall of separation" (Ephesians 2:14).

"Therefore, having been justified by faith, we have peace with God through our Lord Jesus Christ" (Romans 5:1).

Our ability to have peace with God was achieved by Christ upon the cross. This is now the message we are to take to the world: that they, just like us, can have peace with God. As messengers of peace we must seek to be at peace and communicate peace to all people even when they do not show peace to us (cf. Rom. 12:18). If we ever find ourselves communicating anything else we are failing to deliver the correct message (cf. Rom. 14:19).

Peace of God

'And the peace of God, which surpasses all understanding, will guard your hearts and minds through Christ Jesus" (Philippians 4:7).

Once we have peace with God, we know there is nothing else to fear, for nothing can ever separate us from God (cf. Rom. 8:31-39), this is what we call the peace of God. The peace of God is essential to effectively reaching the world due to the fall. As His witnesses, we are at war with the powers of this world and because of this, taking the gospel to the world means facing trials and tribulations. Christ came to earth knowing what His task would mean, humiliation and death upon a cross. He tells us that we too must go through struggles (cf. John 16:33). It is the peace of God that gives us the courage and strength to continue in our task.

SALT & LIGHT: Ask God to comfort your heart and give you His peace that you may share the gospel (peace with God) to the people around you.

ONE LAST THOUGHT: We must have peace with God (comes through salvation) to have the peace of God (comes through sanctification). We have been entrusted with both through the Great Commission.

Day 26:
Being Like Our Master: Giving Comfort to Those Who Mourn

Isaiah 61:2b-3a, "To comfort all who mourn, to console those who mourn in Zion, to give them beauty for ashes, the oil of joy for mourning, the garment of praise for the spirit of heaviness;"

Journal:

Part of our responsibility in fulfilling the Great Commission is to comfort those who mourn. We do so by helping them understand the resurrected Christ. Jesus quoted this passage and applied it to Himself (cf. Luke 4:16-21). The historical background of this passage is about the "Year of Jubilee" as described in Leviticus 25. The Hebrew people observed a "sabbatical year" every seven years in which they allowed the land to rest. However, after seven of those sabbatical years (i.e. 49 years), they were to celebrate the 50th year as the "Year of Jubilee." It was during that year that all debts were canceled, land was returned to the original owners, and slaves were set free. It was a time of rejoicing and celebration for a new beginning.

When we consider this passage in light of Christ, we are experiencing the joy of a spiritual "Year of Jubilee." Christ has given us beauty for ashes (a symbol of mourning). He has anointed us with the oil of the Holy Spirit. He has given us His robe of righteousness to wear! He has cancelled our debt of sin and freed us from the bondage of sin!

Every day is a "Year of Jubilee" because of Christ. However, there was still much work to be done during the "Year of Jubilee." The Hebrew people took this time to rebuild, make repairs, and of course restore their land. They even worked with the Gentiles to care for the flocks and herds! Likewise, there is much work for us in sharing the good news of the resurrected Christ with those who are mourning.

SALT & LIGHT: Whatever has caused you to mourn this year, know that Christ offers comfort. Know that He has already brought victory for you and that you are living in a "Year of Jubilee."

ONE LAST THOUGHT: You have been entrusted with the responsibility to find those who are mourning (lost without Christ) and offer them the oil of joy (the Holy Spirit) and the garment of praise (the atonement of Christ).

Day 27:

Being Like Our Master: Bringing Glory to God

Isaiah 61:3b, "that they might be called trees of righteousness, the planting of the LORD, that He might be glorified."

Journal:

In Luke 4, Jesus identified Himself as the fulfillment of Isaiah's prophecy given in Isaiah 61. Jesus' revelation to the crowd not only fulfilled the prophecy but it also served as a mission statement for His life. Jesus' mission was to be one of love, compassion, shepherding, servitude and salvation. He would take on the worst that the world had to offer and in return deliver mercy, grace and love. Why would He do something so selfless? He did it for the honor and glory of His Father.

Many times Jesus said or implied that He could do nothing that He did not see the Father do. Jesus learned the proper way to live and minister by keeping His eyes on God the Father. A life lived in that fashion brings about glory and honor to God.

I once saw a young child at a church event wearing a shirt with the slogan, "Living my life to make God famous." Think about that for a minute... what if we all lived in such a way to make God famous and to take a backseat to our own desires? What if our works and deeds and mercies and compassions were all done with the end goal of bringing glory to the King of Kings?

We are not without a roadmap to help us live such a life. The life and ministry of Jesus as recorded throughout the Gospels reveals how we each can make our lives count for the purpose of glorifying God. God knew that we could never do this on our own. So, he gave us the Holy Spirit to be our guide. With His help, we can be trees of righteousness and bring glory to the God who created us.

SALT & LIGHT: God, guide my life so that it might bring glory and honor to You.

ONE LAST THOUGHT: What if our works and deeds and mercies and compassions were all done with the end goal of bringing glory to the King of Kings?

Day 28:

Being Like Our Master: The Mount Vision

John 20:21-22, "So Jesus said to them again, 'Peace to you! As the Father has sent Me, I also send you.' And when He had said this, He breathed on them, and said to them, 'Receive the Holy Spirit.'"

Journal:

_____
_____
_____
_____
_____
_____
_____
_____
_____
_____
_____
_____
_____
_____
_____
_____
_____
_____
_____
_____
_____
_____
_____

This week we have examined the authority of the Great Commission, "to be ambassadors for Christ." We have been chosen by God to be His ambassadors. "Now then, we are ambassadors for Christ, as though God were pleading through us: we implore you on Christ's behalf, be reconciled to God" (2 Cor. 5:20). The Holy Spirit's indwelling of the disciple is essential for the Great Commission to be effective. We are not representing ourselves, but Christ who lives in us! We must remember that it is the Holy Spirit who convicts of sin (cf. John 16:8). It is the Spirit who does the work of regeneration and renewing (cf. Titus 3:5). It is even the Spirit that enables us to confess Jesus as Lord (cf. 1 Corinthians 12:3).

Jesus declared, "All authority has been given to Me in heaven and on earth" Matthew 28:18. It is with this authority that Jesus pronounced the Great Commission. Furthermore, it is with the indwelling of the Holy Spirit that empowered the disciples to do the work of the Great Commission.

As Christians, we are called to "walk by the Spirit" and not according to the flesh (cf. Galatians 5:13-26). When we walk according to the Spirit of God, we are not controlled by our own desires. Our own desires are described as "the flesh" and it does not produce the fruit that God desires in our lives. In fact, it produces a fruit that is in complete opposition to the fruit produced by the Spirit. We "walk by the Spirit" when the desires of God are stronger than the desires of our flesh. Therefore, when we "walk by the Spirit" it produces Christ-likeness in our lives.

When we are "led by the Spirit" (God's initiative), we are then to "walk by the Spirit" (our response). The Holy Spirit leads us and we respond with obedience. When we walk according to the flesh, we produce the works of the flesh. We are not following God's desires. When we walk according the Spirit, we produce the fruit of the Spirit. We can never fulfill the Great Commission of our own authority. Apart from the indwelling work of the Holy Spirit, our own flesh would oppose the Great Commission. We must be careful not to hinder the work of the Holy Spirit in the life of a church.

SALT & LIGHT: Lord, help me each day to be alert to the activity of God and to walk in obedience to the Spirit's leading. Amen.

ONE LAST THOUGHT: Missional living is a daily call to be led by the Spirit (God's activity) and walk by the Spirit (our response).

Small Group Guide for Week 4: **The Authority**

WELCOME: If you have new members, take time to briefly introduce yourselves.

PRAYER: Take some time to pray for your group before your begin the lesson.

SPIRITUAL HABITS: Take some time to review the Spiritual HABITS. Ask how the group is doing keeping up with the daily devotions (this is the "H" in HABITS). Ask if anyone needs Scripture Memory Key Tags (this is the "B" in HABITS).

TOPIC TEASER: "Being Like Our Master"
In what ways are you most like Jesus? Explain.
In what ways are you least like Jesus? Explain.

READ THE SCRIPTURES:
Ask for a volunteer in the group to read John 20:21-22. Consider reading it a few times from different translations.

STUDY THE SCRIPTURES:
What is the *authority* of the Great Commission?

DISCUSSION:
Use the space below to take notes on your discussion of the devotions.

_____
_____
_____
_____
_____
_____
_____
_____
_____
_____
_____
_____
_____
_____
_____
_____
_____
_____
_____
_____
_____

APPLY THE SCRIPTURES:
A passage of Scripture has a specific meaning, but has many points of application. As a group, discuss how you have been challenged to live missionally as a result of your time in God's Word this week?

PERSONAL

MY PERSONAL ACTION STEP:
What do you think God wants you to do as a result of your studies and small group discussion this week?

_____
_____
_____

MISSIONS COORDINATOR

MISSIONS PROJECT:
Ask your Small Group Missions Coordinator to give an update. Write down some key details here:

_____
_____
_____
_____
_____
_____
_____

SNEAK PEEK:
Next week we will focus on the *strategy* of the Great Commission.

PRAYER REQUESTS & PRAYER:
Take prayer requests and close in prayer.

_____
_____
_____
_____
_____
_____
_____
_____
_____

LEADER NOTE:
Dismiss your group, but make yourself available to anyone who has questions.

Week 5

Acts: The Strategy I

This week we will focus on Luke's second-volume account of the Great Commission and the strategy for making disciples. God's strategy for the Great Commission is to expand outward.

"But you shall receive power when the Holy Spirit has come upon you; and you shall be witnesses to Me in Jerusalem, and in all Judea and Samaria, and to the end of the earth."
Acts 1:8

Day 29:
Expanding the Kingdom of God

Acts 1:8, "But you shall receive power when the Holy Spirit has come upon you; and you shall be witnesses to Me in Jerusalem, and in all Judea and Samaria, and to the end of the earth."

In Acts 1:8, we find God's strategy for building His Kingdom: going. Even though the emphasis in Matthew's account is the verb "make disciples," it too begins with the word "go." This is because making disciples is impossible without going in God's plan, especially when the whole world is our target. Staying where we are means we have limited opportunities to share the gospel. Just as Jesus left heaven to come to us, we must leave the comfort of our routines to reach others.

Consider these words and their definitions...

> **cen-trip-e-tal force**: a force that acts on a body moving in a circular path and is directed toward the center around which the body is moving.

> **cen-trif-u-gal force**: an apparent force that acts outward on a body moving around a center, arising from the body's inertia.

In the Old Testament, God established a centralized location of worship with the people of Israel. The Israelites were meant to be an example to the rest of the world, drawing people from the nations to them (centripetal). However, with the Great Commission, God established a new pattern. The list in Acts begins where the old system ended, in Jerusalem. The disciples were to begin where they were and what they knew well; to the people that they belonged and the ones they knew best. From there they were to expand outward to people less and less like themselves with each step. Instead of the world coming to them in order to hear about God, they were to take the message to

Journal:

_____
_____
_____
_____
_____
_____
_____
_____
_____
_____
_____
_____
_____
_____
_____
_____
_____
_____
_____
_____
_____
_____
_____
_____
_____
_____
_____
_____
_____

the world (centrifugal).

In the first seven chapters of Acts we find the church staying in Jerusalem. We are told that they visited the temple every day:

"So continuing daily with one accord in the temple, and breaking bread from house to house, they ate their food with gladness and simplicity of heart, praising God and having favor with all the people. And the Lord added to the church daily those who were being saved" (Acts 2:46-47).

But, remember that Jesus told them to stay in Jerusalem only until they received the Spirit, not indefinitely (cf. Luke 24:49). At first the disciples encounter a great deal of success. However, throughout these first few chapters we also find the church encountering greater and greater persecution as they continue to stay in Jerusalem, they forgot to move outwards. It is this persecution that eventually forces believers to move out of Jerusalem and into the wider world (notice Luke tells us where they went: Judea and Samaria (cf. Acts 8:1), the next two spheres mentioned in Acts 1:8).

Part of the problem was their expectations. Several times in the gospel accounts, the disciples ask Jesus when He is going to restore Israel to its former glory. The Apostles expected Jesus to reinstate the kingdom of Israel. In fact, even after His resurrection they still inquired about it:

"Therefore, when they had come together, they asked Him, saying, 'Lord, will You at this time restore the kingdom to Israel?' And He said to them, 'It is not for you to know times or seasons which the Father has put in His own authority. But you shall receive power when the Holy Spirit has come upon you; and you shall be witnesses to Me in Jerusalem, and in all Judea and Samaria, and to the end of the earth'" (Acts 1:6-8).

What they did not understand was that God was changing the system. To make this impossible to miss for future generations, God eventually had the Romans completely destroy the temple, the center of the old system. With no center left to draw people to, Christianity had no choice but to expand outward. While we carry out our mission to spread the gospel to the world, we must be careful that we aren't trying to build the wrong Kingdom too. Sometimes we confuse our own prosperity for the prosperity in the Kingdom of Heaven. However, one does not equal the other. The kingdom of God does not equal the kingdom of Israel and, therefore, it is not confined to the borders of Israel. Neither is it to equal our own prosperity and be confined to the local church. Because of this our focus cannot be limited to ourselves. We must be centrifugal in our outlooks, always looking to spread God's influence to new places and peoples.

SALT & LIGHT: Where has your focus been? Have you been centripetally focused or centrifugally focused?

ONE LAST THOUGHT: Remember that God's strategy is to spread the gospel outward, not draw the world to us.

Day 30:

Expanding the Kingdom of God: To Our City

Acts 1:8, "But you shall receive power when the Holy Spirit has come upon you; and you shall be witnesses to Me in <u>Jerusalem</u>, and in all Judea and Samaria, and to the end of the earth."

Journal:

Acts 1:8 is a verse that commands us to spread the gospel, simple yet something we rarely do. Is it just the pastor's job to spread the gospel to our city? The answer is simple: no. Pastors do have a responsibility of spreading and teaching the gospel, but the verse clearly states that when the Holy Spirit has come upon *you*. That means that all people who have a relationship with Jesus are called to share the gospel. We must get out of the mindset as believers that say, "That's the pastor's job." If we truly want to see our city come to know Christ then we must *all* be on mission and *all* be taking the gospel to each person. We must truly change our city for Christ.

Think about church growth and how churches grow. When some churches "grow," they may do so by drawing believers out of less vital churches. This can be a good thing if these Christians are being better discipled and if their gifts are being effectively deployed. Nevertheless, if this is the primary means of "growth," then the overall body of Christ in the city is not growing; it is simply "reshuffling the deck". Reaching an entire city takes more than trading membership. Changing the city with the gospel takes a movement. We cannot simply move others from one church to another, we must be willing to leave our comfort zone and go into the community. The lost do not look for the church unless (1) someone invites them or (2) tragedy strikes in their life. Let's not wait until tragedy occurs before we invite others!

So how does a gospel movement occur in our city? The first thing we must do is: allow God to work and not begin to interfere with His plan for our city. This means that God can do a lot more than we could ever imagine. God can open the hearts of individuals to the Word of God. He can also open the culture to the gospel as a whole. It is our responsibility to listen to God when He calls us to reach out to our community. We must be obedient to His calling. Many times we tend to ignore a situation that God is calling us to because we are scared. We need to have faith and trust Him in these times if we want to reach our city. While it will be hard to do in many cases, it will be worth it. I want to ask a simple question that may help you in sharing the gospel. "If you knew someone close to you was not a believer, wouldn't you want to see them in Heaven one day?

It is important that we begin in our city, that we look toward our neighbor in love and minister to them. That we truly begin to look toward God and ask, who can I lead to You today? We have the Holy Spirit within us and we have a God that is moving within our city. Let's be part of that and allow God to show us those who need Him today.

SALT & LIGHT: God, show me someone today that I can lead to You, not simply invite to church, but someone that needs to hear of Your love. God give me the eyes and heart to see those in need of You, then give me the courage and strength to share Your love with them today. Amen.

ONE LAST THOUGHT: We cannot produce a gospel movement without the work of the Holy Spirit. A movement is empowered and blessed by God's Spirit.

Day 31:
Expanding the Kingdom of God: To Our County

Acts 1:8, "But you shall receive power when the Holy Spirit has come upon you; and you shall be witnesses to Me in Jerusalem, and in all <u>Judea</u> and Samaria, and to the end of the earth."

Journal:

_____
_____
_____
_____
_____
_____
_____
_____
_____
_____
_____
_____
_____
_____
_____
_____
_____
_____
_____
_____
_____
_____
_____
_____
_____

Jerusalem is the primary city in the nation of Israel and rests within a region called Judea (a Greek and Roman adaptation of the Hebrew name "Judah"). Prior to the Babylonian conquest the region was called Judah. It's not a county or a state in the sense we would use those words. However, the application for us is the same. We are to begin in our "Jerusalem" (i.e. Mount Sterling) and spread the gospel into the larger community in which we live. For our context, we might consider Montgomery County as our "Judea."

While the reasons might be many and varied, a lot of churches have developed a "Field of Dreams" mentality of ministry and missions: build a better program or larger building and people will come. However, that's not God's strategy for the church to grow. God's strategy is to expand the kingdom through communities and mobilizing the church. This is the heart of our hashtag campaign: #forMoCo. We want our community to know that we exist *for* them. Our church facilities should never be built for ourselves, our facilities should be built for our community and to help us accomplish the Great Commission. When our church gymnasiums become exclusive for church members then we have missed our missional opportunity to reach the community in which we live. This is why we must never become attached to rooms, furniture, or even our programs! All of those things may need to change to help us better fulfill the Great Commission!

The best examples of our church being "for Montgomery County" are seen through our small groups. We have a small group that hosts an annual "teacher appreciation dinner" for a different school in our community each year. Our KidMin (i.e. children's ministry) small groups collect money to provide beds for children in Montgomery County and the eastern part of our state. Another small group is discussing an appreciation dinner for firefighters, police officers, and medical personnel. Our Kids Camp (VBS) is one of our largest community events of the year in which a high percentage of our church volunteer their time to let our community know that we are for them!

The hashtag campaign (#forMoCo) is not about the pastors doing the work of ministry. It is not built around a personality or even a single program. It is built upon the mindset that our entire church is committed to missional living!

SALT & LIGHT: What can you and your small group do to demonstrate that you are #forMoCo?

ONE LAST THOUGHT: The hashtag campaign is not about being "tech savvy," it is about being missional in our community!

Day 32:

Expanding the Kingdom of God: To Our State

Acts 1:8, "But you shall receive power when the Holy Spirit has come upon you; and you shall be witnesses to Me in Jerusalem, and in all Judea and Samaria, and to the end of the earth."

Journal:

_____
_____
_____
_____
_____
_____
_____
_____
_____
_____
_____
_____
_____
_____
_____
_____
_____
_____
_____
_____
_____
_____
_____
_____
_____
_____
_____

Jesus' instructions in Matthew 28 and Acts 1 carry with them the implication that we are to begin our ministries close to home but they should expand to all parts of the world. How effective would our ministries be if we failed to share our faith with those closest to us but yet travel great distances to share it with strangers? One might argue that we couldn't be effective at all.

God desires for us to be equipped and able to share His Good News with our families, neighbors and those we don't even know. We may learn and apply our ministry skills close to home but that is just the beginning. God intends for our ministries to know no bounds.

God has given a wonderful vision to our pastor and He has entrusted a great work to His church at First Baptist Church Mount Sterling. That vision and work is to see that the Eastern portion of our state is reached with the Good News of Jesus Christ. Despite the fact that it lies soundly within the "Bible Belt" boundaries, the Appalachian region of our state is a huge mission field.

The commonwealth of Kentucky is made up of 120 counties. Roughly 40 of those counties are located East of Interstate 75 and those counties help make up the Appalachian region and its foothills. Despite having thousands of established churches, the region is inhabited primarily by unsaved people. It is a region full of poverty, drug addiction, high unemployment, and hopelessness. Imagine the impact and the resources that could be saved if Christians throughout Kentucky would make it their priority to share the hope of Jesus with these people.

While Samaria is not a "state" in the sense that Kentucky is a state, the people of the Appalachian region in our state are our neighbors, just as the Samaritans were neighbors to those in Judea.

If Kentucky is our "Samaria," are you ready to heed Jesus' command? We cannot delay in our efforts to reach the lost in our state!

SALT & LIGHT: God, please equip and inspire me to be a light to this great state. Help me to expand your Kingdom in Kentucky.

ONE LAST THOUGHT: God desires us to be equipped and able to share His good news with our families, neighbors, and those we don't even know.

Day 33:
Expanding the Kingdom of God: To Our World

Acts 1:8, "But you shall receive power when the Holy Spirit has come upon you; and you shall be witnesses to Me in Jerusalem, and in all Judea and Samaria, and to <u>the end of the earth</u>."

Journal:

_____
_____
_____
_____
_____
_____

_____
_____
_____
_____
_____
_____
_____

_____
_____
_____
_____
_____
_____
_____

_____
_____
_____
_____

Why in the world would you go overseas to share the gospel when there are so many here who haven't accepted Christ? That question is one that I have heard repeatedly since my first mission trip. One has several options by which to adequately respond to such a question. Our church has recently developed a three-year plan to partner with long-term missionaries in Mongolia, so I will focus the discussion around that context.

First, less than 3% of the entire population of Mongolia professes to be Christian. What was painfully obvious to those of us who were blessed to be part of our first trip to Mongolia, is that this is not due to a hostile attitude toward the gospel. Rather, it is due in large part to the fact that many there, especially outside the capital, have never even heard of Jesus. They have never rejected the gospel, because they have never heard the gospel. Paul speaks plainly about those in this situation in Romans 10:13b-14 when he writes, "Everyone who calls on the name of the Lord will be saved. How, then, can they call on the one they have not believed in? And how can they believe in the one of whom they have not heard? And how can they hear without someone preaching to them? And how can anyone preach unless they are sent? As it is written: 'How beautiful are the feet of those who bring good news.'"

Second, we are not all going at the same time. The model that is presented in the book of Acts shows the church sending out small groups of people to fulfill the Great Commission to the ends of the earth (cf. Acts

13). The rest of the church, then, continued on in their normal location and it is evident that they continued to spread the gospel in their current setting. On this year's trip, we have just around 3% of our church members who will be going to Mongolia. That leaves, of course, 97% of the church to continue to work in fulfilling the Great Commission here at home.

Third, in Montgomery County there are over 100 churches. Our county, and much of our nation, is saturated with churches. One living near me, could literally walk to several churches in about 15 minutes, though surely we would drive. In Mongolia, it might take a full day's drive to get to the nearest church, and even that would be a near impossibility for most because 90% do not own a vehicle.

Finally and most importantly, we go overseas because it is what we are commanded to do. More than any of the practical reasons listed above, we must go to the ends of the earth because Jesus told us specifically to do so. The Bible does not suggest that if we get around to it, we live out Acts 1:8. Living out the Great Commission in its entirety is precisely what it means to follow Christ (cf. John 14:15). If we love Him, we must obey Him. If we desire to be His disciple, we must take up our crosses and follow.

Many people will never be involved in missions and evangelism regardless of the location. The easy way out is to simply say that one doesn't feel called to do those things. What is clear, however, through the Scriptures is that the call already exists for us all. We must never wait on a thundering voice from the heavens to push us toward spreading the gospel. The words of Christ, through the Scriptures, are that very voice to all believers.

William Booth, the founder of the Salvation Army, said it well when he wrote,

'Not called!' did you say?

'Not heard the call,' I think you should say.

Put your ear down to the Bible, and hear Him bid you go and pull sinners out of the fire of sin. Put your ear down to the burdened, agonized heart of humanity, and listen to its pitiful wail for help. Go stand by the gates of hell, and hear the damned entreat you to go to their father's house and bid their brothers and sisters and servants and masters not to come there. Then look Christ in the face — whose mercy you have professed to obey — and tell Him whether you will join heart and soul and body and circumstances in the march to publish His mercy to the world.

Our calling has already been laid before us. From our next-door neighbors to the very uttermost parts of the planet, we must be focused on making disciples for the sake of Christ!

SALT & LIGHT: God help me in every aspect of my life to live missionally. Help me to be burdened for the souls of people who I encounter every day. Fill me with the power of the Holy Spirit and help me to publish Your mercy to this lost and dying world!

ONE LAST THOUGHT: Though missions can, and does, take on many different forms in the life of a Christian, missions is not optional. He has called us all. How will we respond?

Day 34:
Expanding the Kingdom of God: To the Despised and Hated

Acts 1:8, "But you shall receive power when the Holy Spirit has come upon you; and you shall be witnesses to Me in Jerusalem, and in all Judea and Samaria, and to the end of the earth."

One of the regions mentioned in Acts 1:8 stands out more than the others given the history of Israel: Samaria. While this can be seen as a neighboring region, it also has another meaning. Jews and Samaritans despised each other.

The Samaritans were the descendants of the poorest people left behind by the Assyrians when they took the northern kingdom of Israel into captivity and the Gentile nations they brought in to settle the land. They had continued to worship God, but also welcomed the foreign gods that the foreign nations brought with them. Later when the southern kingdom of Judah returned from their captivity in Babylon, the Samaritans fought their reintegration and rebuilding of Jerusalem's walls. This troubled history makes it all that more poignant that Jesus chose a Samaritan in his parable about who our neighbors are. It is interesting that the man who Jesus was talking to can't even bring himself to say the word "Samaritan" but says "the one who showed him mercy" instead (cf. Luke 10:37).

God included Samaria in the list of where the gospel was to be taken because we need a push to reach out to those with whom we have nothing in common. Not the ones on the other side of the world, those we have no problem reaching (at least for that week or two we go on a mission trip to visit), but those that live across the street and don't look or act like us. These are the people we need extra motivation to reach because they are the biggest threat to our own comfort and

Journal:

_____
_____
_____
_____
_____
_____
_____
_____
_____
_____
_____
_____
_____
_____
_____
_____
_____
_____
_____
_____
_____
_____
_____
_____
_____
_____
_____
_____
_____

complacency. We know just enough about them to know they don't think like us and, therefore, will challenge what we believe and cause us to adapt our strategies in order to reach them. As creatures of habit we want to resist change. This is especially true in our religious lives. We don't like questioning how we have always done things. However, sometimes we must change in order to reach new people, as Peter learned:

"The next day, as they went on their journey and drew near the city, Peter went up on the housetop to pray, about the sixth hour. Then he became very hungry and wanted to eat; but while they made ready, he fell into a trance and saw heaven opened and an object like a great sheet bound at the four corners, descending to him and let down to the earth. In it were all kinds of four-footed animals of the earth, wild beasts, creeping things, and birds of the air. And a voice came to him, 'Rise, Peter; kill and eat.' But Peter said, 'Not so, Lord! For I have never eaten anything common or unclean.' And a voice *spoke* to him again the second time, 'What God has cleansed you must not call common.' This was done three times. And the object was taken up into heaven again" (Acts 10:9-16).

Reaching new people may mean we have to offer additional worship services. It may mean that our church focuses less on the desires of our members and more on the needs of the community. It may mean less face time with our pastors because there are so many new faces. At the end of the day these sacrifices to our comforts are worth it when we see lives changed and the kingdom of God expanded. After all, that is our mission, not to stay comfortable with our friends.

SALT & LIGHT: Ask God to reveal to you the people you have been avoiding and what you can begin to do to reach out to them with the gospel.

ONE LAST THOUGHT: We are commanded to share the gospel with everyone around us, even those who are despised and hated.

Day 35:

Expanding the Kingdom of God: The Mount Vision

Acts 1:8, "But you shall receive power when the Holy Spirit has come upon you; and you shall be witnesses to Me in Jerusalem, and in all Judea and Samaria, and to the end of the earth."

Journal:

_____
_____
_____
_____
_____
_____
_____
_____
_____
_____
_____
_____
_____
_____
_____
_____
_____
_____
_____
_____
_____
_____
_____
_____
_____

This week we have examined the strategy of the Great Commission, "to start near and go far." Considering the original context of this passage, you are most likely the product of the Great Commission as it has reached "the ends of the earth." However, if we seek to apply the principles here, we should begin local (Jerusalem), expand outward (Judea), reach those who are different from ourselves (Samaria), and go to all nations (ends of the earth).

Within the context of the vision for our local church, we should begin with our own city (our Jerusalem). That's why we do things such as door-to-door evangelism, Kids Camp, and community concerts. These are opportunities for our church to engage the city. Notice the smallest people group we are called to reach is an entire city!

Second, we should continue with a desire to reach the county in which we live (our Judea). Many in our community have some idea of what the church is against, but they would have a hard time identifying what the church is for! We want our county to know we are *FOR* them! We want strong schools; we support law enforcement, firefighters, and the many others who serve our community. This is why we host events such as teacher appreciation luncheons.

Third, we want to share the gospel with those who are our neighbors, but may challenge us to cross cultural barriers (our Samaria). East Kentucky has often been looked down upon by much of the state. God has uniquely placed us in such a place to reach them with the gospel, not to "look down on them."

Finally, we want to reach the ends of the earth by taking international mission trips like those to Mongolia (our ends of the earth). It's important that we do not become so inwardly focused that we fail to go to hard to reach places.

Notice the passage does not read, "you will be my witnesses in Jerusalem, THEN in all Judea, THEN Samaria, THEN to the ends of the earth." No! The word is AND! The Bible is making a clear command through the Great Commission that we are not to do one THEN the next, but ALL of them are to occur at the same time! What an incredible task for the local church to expand the Kingdom of God!

SALT & LIGHT: How can you become more involved in reaching your city, county, state, and world for Christ? Can you provide an actionable step for all four areas?

ONE LAST THOUGHT: Missional living is making an impact not just locally, but in all areas at the same time!

Small Group Guide for Week 5: **The Strategy**

WELCOME: If you have new members, take time to briefly introduce yourselves.

PRAYER: Take some time to pray for your group before your begin the lesson.

SPIRITUAL HABITS: Take some time to review the Spiritual HABITS. Ask how the group is doing keeping up with the daily devotions (this is the "H" in HABITS). Ask if anyone needs Scripture Memory Key Tags (this is the "B" in HABITS).

TOPIC TEASER: "Expanding the Kingdom"
In what ways is it easier to share the gospel on a mission trip as opposed to your own community? Why is it important for our church to take the gospel to eastern Kentucky?

READ THE SCRIPTURES:
Ask for a volunteer in the group to read Acts 1:8. Consider reading it a few times from different translations.

STUDY THE SCRIPTURES:
What is the *strategy* of the Great Commission?

DISCUSSION:
Use the space below to take notes on your discussion of the devotions.

_____
_____
_____
_____
_____
_____
_____
_____
_____
_____
_____
_____
_____
_____
_____
_____
_____
_____
_____
_____

APPLY THE SCRIPTURES:

A passage of Scripture has a specific meaning, but has many points of application. As a group, discuss how you have been challenged to live missionally as a result of your time in God's Word this week?

PERSONAL

MY PERSONAL ACTION STEP:
What do you think God wants you to do as a result of your studies and small group discussion this week?

_____
_____
_____

MISSIONS COORDINATOR

MISSIONS PROJECT:
Ask your Small Group Missions Coordinator to give an update. Write down some key details here:

_____
_____
_____
_____
_____
_____
_____

SNEAK PEEK:
Next week we will focus on the *strategy* of the Great Commission.

PRAYER REQUESTS & PRAYER:
Take prayer requests and close in prayer.

_____
_____
_____
_____
_____
_____
_____
_____
_____

LEADER NOTE:
Dismiss your group, but make yourself available to anyone who has questions.

Week 6

Acts: The Strategy II

This week we will focus on Luke's second-volume account of the Great Commission and the strategy for making disciples. God's strategy is to mobilize the local church to reach beyond their borders.

"But you shall receive power when the Holy Spirit has come upon you; and you shall be witnesses to Me in Jerusalem, and in all Judea and Samaria, and to the end of the earth."
Acts 1:8

Day 36:
Mobilizing the Church: Church Planting

Acts 14:21-23, "And when they had preached the gospel to that city and made many disciples, they returned to Lystra, Iconium, and Antioch, strengthening the souls of the disciples, exhorting them to continue in the faith, and saying, 'We must through many tribulations enter the kingdom of God.' So when they had appointed elders in every church, and prayed with fasting, they commended them to the Lord in whom they had believed."

Every good strategy needs equally good tactics to implement it. God's strategy for reaching the nations is an ever-expanding circle. But, what does that mean in the day-to-day steps of carrying out that strategy? In chapter 14 of Acts we get a glimpse of Paul's tactics for carrying out God's strategy for reaching the lost world: church planting.

In Acts 14, we find Paul and Barnabas traveling around the Iconium region of Asia Minor establishing new churches. The churches that we find Paul planting are house churches, what we might call small groups. Only later, once there were enough of these house churches would they be organized into something more akin to what we now think of as a church with appointed pastors.

The real strength in this model is its fluidity and adaptability. It allowed the apostles to react to the response they received from the communities. If the people responded positively to the gospel, they were free to stay longer and give ongoing support to the new believers. However, if they were met with resistance, they could move on quickly to the next area. Either way, this method of constant moving on to new areas allowed them to more easily discern where God was working. Wherever there is growth (whether or not there is also opposition) is where we find Paul and Barnabas lingering. This confirms that God is indeed at work in the area before investing a lot of resources that may be more

Journal:

productive elsewhere. God works in His own timing and this applies to establishing churches as well. In our over-eagerness to do something for God, we may seek to rush through the steps of planting a church too soon. Unlike "Field of Dreams," just because we build it doesn't necessary mean they will come. It is important that we go where God is already working, not for us to go somewhere and then ask God to show up.

Not only do we find Paul and Barnabas constantly going to new areas, but we also find them revisiting places they had already been. Acts 14 tells us this is for the purposes of strengthening and encouraging the new believers in their faith. Carrying out our commission requires us to establish long-term relationships. Visiting a place one time is not enough. Only repeated and consistent engagement allows time to teach people to be disciples. Again, this is why small groups are so effective. They foster long-term relationships with people. Relationships that go well beyond the casual level we often encounter on Sunday mornings. They allow believers to make lasting spiritual investments in other people's lives.

Finally, Paul and Barnabas also help establish spiritual leadership in the new churches once they have had time to grow. Eventually this led to the appointment of permanent pastors for the new churches, as with Timothy in Ephesus, and the recruitment of missionaries from the new churches to begin the process all over again. By waiting until the house churches had grown, it allowed time for these leaders to develop.

SALT & LIGHT: Small groups are an important part of church planting and, therefore, an important part of the vision of our church. If you are not currently part of an active small group, begin taking steps to invest in the vision of the church by joining one today.

ONE LAST THOUGHT: Many churches have become so inwardly focused that they have not made any effort to plant churches in decades!

_____
_____
_____
_____
_____
_____
_____
_____
_____
_____
_____
_____
_____
_____
_____
_____
_____
_____
_____
_____
_____
_____
_____
_____
_____
_____
_____
_____
_____
_____

Day 37:
Mobilizing the Church: Obstacles

Acts 14:21-23, "And when they had preached the gospel to that city and made many disciples, they returned to Lystra, Iconium, and Antioch, strengthening the souls of the disciples, exhorting them to continue in the faith, and saying, 'We must through many tribulations enter the kingdom of God.' So when they had appointed elders in every church, and prayed with fasting, they commended them to the Lord in whom they had believed."

Journal:

No one likes to encounter trials, but Scripture makes it clear that tribulations are a necessary part of a believer's life and mission. The new disciples in Antioch, Iconium, and Lystra had just witnessed Paul and Barnabas face overwhelming opposition. In Antioch, the new disciples witnessed opposition to everything Paul and Barnabas shared. The great opposition forced them to "shake the dust from their feet" and move on to Iconium. Likewise, in Iconium they faced enough opposition that forced them to move on to Lystra. In Lystra, Paul and Barnabas went from being embraced as gods to being stoned within an inch of their lives and tossed outside of the city walls.

However, far from being bitter and disheartened by this opposition, Paul used it to strengthen the faith of the disciples that had witnessed it. This is because God uses trials, "And not only *that*, but we also glory in tribulations, knowing that tribulation produces perseverance; and perseverance, character; and character, hope" (Romans 5:3-4).

Beyond building character, God uses trials to guide us as well. At times it is difficult to know if we are on the right path or not. The busyness of life can make it hard to hear God's voice. This can become even more difficult when we begin to encounter obstacles. We tend to look for reasons we are facing the trials. However, we must remember that not every obstacle is because of something negative (cf. John 9:1-5). The trials we encounter can be road signs. If the path we are on is God's will, then we can be sure that Satan will place as many obstacles as possible along that path to deter us. God has the strength to overcome every obstacle that comes across our path; sometimes we simply need to keep moving forward in order for Him to do so. In fact, if we find life rolling by easy and carefree then we can be relatively assured that we are nowhere near God's path.

"But when the Jews saw the multitudes, they were filled with envy; and contradicting and blaspheming, they opposed the things spoken by Paul. Then Paul and Barnabas grew bold and said, "It was necessary that the word of God should be spoken to you first; but since you reject it, and judge yourselves unworthy of everlasting life, behold, we turn to the Gentiles" (Acts 13:45-56).

Sometimes, however, obstacles may mean that we need to move on and change our focus. In fact, it was this kind of obstacle that eventually lead Paul and Barnabas to focus their efforts to reaching Gentiles. Likewise, Paul and Barnabas frequency faced opposition so great they had to move on to the next city. God wanted them to take a detour for a while. Many times they were able to return later to all these cities and do work, but God wanted them to wait for His timing and not theirs (cf. Rom. 1:13).

The obvious question is, "How can I tell the difference?" The answer is simple: discernment. However, using discernment usually isn't so simple. Being able to discern what God is telling us takes both prayer and experience. Since God uses trials to build our character and maturity, the more trials we face the more easily we will be able to understand what He is doing in our lives in the future. Likewise, the trials and experience of other believers around us serve as guidance for us as well. Given there is nothing new under the sun (cf. Ecc. 1:9), we can be confident that we can find others who have faced similar circumstances to ours. We need to seek these people out and learn from their experience.

When trying to determine whether or not trials are confirmation of the correct path or a detour, we should look for confirmation in other believers around us as well. God never gives a vision in isolation. One person may receive it sooner than others, but eventually God will give that same vision to multiple people. The more confirmations the more certain we can be of being on the correct path.

SALT & LIGHT: Lord, help me to keep my eyes open to Your activity in the midst of obstacles. The greater the vision often means the obstacles are going to be greater.

ONE LAST THOUGHT: Just because there is opposition does not mean something is wrong, but it is an alert to inquire what God is doing around you.

Day 38:

Mobilizing the Church: Walking Worthy of the Mission

Luke 9:57-62, "Now it happened as they journeyed on the road, that someone said to Him, 'Lord, I will follow You wherever You go.' And Jesus said to him, 'Foxes have holes and birds of the air have nests, but the Son of Man has nowhere to lay His head.' Then He said to another, 'Follow Me.' But he said, 'Lord, let me first go and bury my father.' Jesus said to him, 'Let the dead bury their own dead, but you go and preach the kingdom of God.' And another also said, 'Lord, I will follow You, but let me first go and bid them farewell who are at my house.' But Jesus said to him, 'No one, having put his hand to the plow, and looking back, is fit for the kingdom of God.'"

Carrying out the Great Commission requires a high commitment level. This is why Christ makes the cost of discipleship clear, "If anyone comes to Me and does not hate his father and mother, wife and children, brothers and sisters, yes, and his own life also, he cannot be My disciple" (Luke 14:26). If we ever find ourselves putting something other than Christ first, we are failing to live up to our calling. As today's passage shows, this includes concerns that may be important to us. Any hesitation on our part, regardless of the ultimate reasoning is unworthy of the task. There are several reasons why this is true.

First, placing other things before Christ leads to distractions.

"And Peter answered Him and said, 'Lord, if it is You, command me to come to You on the water.' So He said, 'Come.' And when Peter had come down out of the boat, he walked on the water to go to Jesus. But when he saw that the wind was boisterous, he was afraid; and beginning to sink he cried out, saying, 'Lord, save me!'" (Matthew 14:28-30).

The minute we take our eyes off of Jesus, we begin to waiver and lose our confidence. We are essentially making ourselves ineffective for the work. Our mission is simple: make disciples. Everything we do is to further this mission.

Journal:

_____
_____
_____
_____
_____
_____
_____
_____
_____
_____
_____
_____
_____
_____
_____
_____
_____
_____
_____
_____
_____
_____
_____

However, over time the other things we do can be elevated to the same level of importance as the primary mission of the church. Over the years a church can confuse the mission with programs and traditions. This includes things like weddings and funerals. These are important things in the lives of the body and can be used to further the mission if allowed to stay in their proper place, but they are never to dictate the function of the church and its resources. The moment we find ourselves neglecting the mission of reaching the lost for any other purpose, we have missed the point and become distracted.

Second, putting something else first leads to division in the body.

"I, therefore, the prisoner of the Lord, beseech you to walk worthy of the calling with which you were called, with all lowliness and gentleness, with longsuffering, bearing with one another in love, endeavoring to keep the unity of the Spirit in the bond of peace. *There is* one body and one Spirit, just as you were called in one hope of your calling; one Lord, one faith, one baptism; one God and Father of all, who *is* above all, and through all, and in you all" (Ephesians 4: 1-6).

To walk worthy of our calling we must have unity through the Spirit. There is only one calling, one Spirit, one Lord, one faith. Christ left a clear mission for His Church. Now, each individual church may have a unique vision to accomplish that mission, and that vision will be singular and developed through the leadership of that particular church. Once that vision has been vetted and decided upon by the leadership of the church, any deviation from that vision is a hindrance to the mission. If the Spirit has given us a clear path to follow, we must follow that path. Everyone has opinions. It's a simple fact of being human. However, allowing differing opinions to lead us down different paths creates division. This cannot be the case in the body of Christ; we must work together through the Spirit if we are to be successful.

Finally, other things cause us to hesitate in our obedience.

"But Jesus said to him, 'No one, having put his hand to the plow, and looking back, is fit for the kingdom of God'" (Luke 9:62).

Jesus made it clear what He thinks of hesitation when it comes to following Him, hesitation makes us unfit for service. That is pretty strong language. Even though something may be important to us personally, if these things hinder the progress of the gospel and reaching others, then they are to be put aside without a second thought. This may seem harsh, but the task at hand is so large and difficult by its very nature, we cannot allow anything from our own lives to hinder it further. Even if we must leave family behind, we do so for the sake of the gospel. If we must sell everything we own to be a missionary in a foreign land, we must do it. For at the end of the day, all that matters is the task ahead of us and those people we will reach through our efforts.

SALT & LIGHT: Ask God to reveal anything that you have allowed to take Christ's place in your life and the strength to remove them so that you can accomplish His plan for your life.

ONE LAST THOUGHT: It is impossible to follow Christ and fulfill the Great Commission without making personal sacrifices.

Day 39:

Mobilizing the Church: Door-to-Door Mission

Luke 24:46-47, "Then He said to them, 'Thus it is written, and thus it was necessary for the Christ to suffer and to rise from the dead the third day, and that repentance and remission of sins should be preached in His name to all nations, beginning at Jerusalem."

Journal:

_____
_____
_____
_____
_____
_____
_____
_____
_____
_____
_____
_____
_____
_____
_____
_____
_____
_____
_____
_____
_____
_____
_____

Door-to-door evangelism was once a vibrant strategy of churches for reaching a community for Christ, but has become discarded by many churches as ineffective. What began during our "40 Days of God's Word" spiritual growth campaign as a commitment to pass out 400 copies of the New Testament grew to become a monthly outreach opportunity called "Door-to-Door Evangelism" (D2D).

Each month we gather to pray for our community and for the homes we will be visiting that day. We pray for God to enable us and allow us to be used by Him to introduce people to Christ. Our goal is simply to give them a copy of the New Testament and seek to engage them in gospel-conversations. We don't have a script, we simply seek an opportunity to share our faith and invite them to church through conversation.

The receptivity of our New Testament gift, invitation to church, and gospel-conversation is surprisingly high. A common misconception people have about door-to-door evangelism is the fear of being met with angry or confrontational people. Personally, I have never had someone lash out, threaten me, or become violent while doing door-to-door evangelism. If fear is preventing you from participating in an evangelistic effort such as D2D, I hope you will lay aside these anxieties to experience the joy of sharing your faith with others.

Each time I engage in evangelism efforts, I am reminded of this principle: It's not about me! Evangelism really is not about us at all. We must remember that the underlying objective of door-to-door evangelism is not for personal gain, but for kingdom impact. Our primary concern is that Christ is known. Our motivation should be grounded in our love for Christ and the community in which He has placed us.

"The real business of life is glorifying God and being used by Him to transform unbelievers into people whose great delight in life is to know and trust Him." -Dave Earley, church planter, seminary professor, and author of "Evangelism Is... How To Share Jesus with Passion and Confidence."

I pray that we all grow in our desire to reach the lost. Sharing our faith with a lost and dying world is an act of worship that brings glory to God. Therefore, it isn't about us.

Door-to-door evangelism is just one of several strategies that can be used to fulfill the Great Commission. It's okay to discard one strategy for another, as long as we continue to take the gospel near and far! It is my prayer that we will all have courage to step out in faith and bring glory to our Father in heaven whenever the opportunity presents itself.

SALT & LIGHT: Ask God to help you share the gospel with the world around you. Also, try to attend a D2D type event at least once in the near future.

ONE LAST THOUGHT: Remember that bringing God glory through the salvation of the lost should always be our motivation anytime we interact with a non-believer.

Day 40:
Mobilizing the Church: The Mount Vision
Matthew 5:41, "And whoever compels you to go one mile, go with him two."

Journal:

This week we have examined the continued strategy of the Great Commission, "to mobilize the church." While there are many ways to take the Great Commission into our community, one thing is abundantly clear... we cannot sit idle. We are a people called to action. We have a God-sized task ahead of us, one that will certainly be met with many obstacles. However, all of us are called to "go the extra mile."

During the time of Christ, Roman soldiers could force others to carry their baggage for one mile. Cyrus, the King of Persia, created a postal system in which couriers could force anyone to carry parcel up to one mile. The Romans used a similar system for their military since their baggage weighed as much as 65 pounds. Those who carried the baggage of a Roman soldier would do so out of obligation and would certainly have built up resentment.

This is truly an example of the authentic disciple. The disciple doesn't simply walk one mile, but likely walks four miles! Keep in mind that the disciple must often return to their point of origin. So, instead of just walking one mile, to "walk the extra mile" means to walk closer to four miles. That's sacrificial living. Furthermore, this type of relational encounter would be a stark contrast for the Roman soldier. Imagine the shock of the soldier when the disciple offers to carry the baggage for another mile. It would open doors for the gospel to be shared. Finally, the attitude of the disciple is being transformed to the attitude of Christ. Instead of built up resentment, the soldier is met with a Christ-follower who is eager to go those extra miles.

It is in the second mile that the Great Commission is fulfilled. Let's mobilize the church and get there as quickly as possible!

SALT & LIGHT: Lord, help me to make personal sacrifices for the sake of the Great Commission. Help me to see the relational opportunities to share the gospel. Help me to be transformed to the image of Christ during the second mile! Amen.

ONE LAST THOUGHT: Missional living is seeking out opportunities to go the second mile.

Small Group Guide for Week 6: **The Strategy II**

WELCOME: If you have new members, take time to briefly introduce yourselves.

PRAYER: Take some time to pray for your group before your begin the lesson.

SPIRITUAL HABITS: Take some time to review the Spiritual HABITS. Ask how the group is doing keeping up with the daily devotions (this is the "H" in HABITS). Ask if anyone needs Scripture Memory Key Tags (this is the "B" in HABITS).

TOPIC TEASER: "Mobilizing the Church"
Review Appendix D, "The 2020 Vision" of our church. What can we do, as a small group, to mobilize the church toward the vision that God has for our church?

READ THE SCRIPTURES:
Ask for a volunteer in the group to read Acts 1:8. Consider reading it a few times from different translations.

STUDY THE SCRIPTURES:
What is the *strategy* of the Great Commission?

DISCUSSION:
Use the space below to take notes on your discussion of the devotions.

_____
_____
_____
_____
_____
_____
_____
_____
_____
_____
_____
_____
_____
_____
_____
_____
_____
_____
_____

APPLY THE SCRIPTURES:
A passage of Scripture has a specific meaning, but has many points of application. As a group, discuss how you have been challenged to live missionally as a result of your time in God's Word this week?

PERSONAL

MY PERSONAL ACTION STEP:
What do you think God wants you to do as a result of your studies and small group discussion this week?

_____
_____
_____

MISSIONS COORDINATOR

MISSIONS PROJECT:
Ask your Small Group Missions Coordinator to give an update. Write down some key details here:

_____
_____
_____
_____
_____
_____
_____

PRAYER REQUESTS & PRAYER:
Take prayer requests and close in prayer.

_____
_____
_____
_____
_____
_____
_____
_____
_____

LEADER NOTE:
Dismiss your group, but make yourself available to anyone who has questions.

40 Days of

Missional Living

Section Three: Epilogue

Epilogue

I hope that the personal devotions, small group involvement, and weekend sermons have challenged you to live missionally. I believe that if our church is going to be the New Testament church that Christ has called us to be, then we must each make a commitment to missional living.

I hope and pray that "40 Days of Missional Living" has helped you see yourself as a missionary in the community in which you live. It is my prayer that each 40 Days Spiritual Growth Campaign we have will encourage those who participate to develop a lifetime of abiding in Christ through time in His word.

I have provided space below for you to personalize your spiritual growth journey over the past 40 days. I hope you will prayerfully write down your thoughts in each area.

Take a moment to consider how God has used this spiritual growth campaign to produce spiritual maturity in your own life.

Before "40 Days of Missional Living" I was struggling with... (Tell what questions you had or life issues you have been struggling with.)

_____
_____
_____

Because of this I've been... (Share how the issue/question has affected you, other relationships, other activities, etc.)

_____
_____
_____

But through the "40 days of Missional Living" I learned, read, saw, heard... (What did God reveal to you through this spiritual growth campaign?)

_____
_____
_____

A big help during this time was... (Tell who helped you and what Bible verse, event, or incident got your attention.)

_____
_____
_____

As a result... (Describe what conclusion you came to as well as any commitments you made.)

_____
_____
_____

Some of the things I learned were... (Detail what you learned about yourself, God, the Bible, others, etc.)

_____
_____
_____

Based on what I've learned I... (Share your current strategy and game plan.)

_____
_____
_____

As a result I... (Tell whether or not you feel equipped to help others with similar issues, questions, etc.)

_____
_____
_____

One of the biggest surprises through the process was... (Tell about your biggest surprise during the lesson, and whether it was good or bad.)

_____
_____
_____

I would love it if you'd pray that I... (Share how others can pray for you.)

_____
_____
_____

Once you have written your thoughts in each area, prayerfully consider sharing your story with others in our church during the "40 Days of Missional Living" Celebrations Worship Service. If so, please email Pastor Christopher Wilson at christopher@fbcmtsterling.com and include "40 Days Testimony" in the subject line.

Abiding in Him,
Pastor Chris Dortch

40 Days of

Missional Living

Section Four: Appendices

APPENDIX A:
How To Become A Christian

God's Purpose for Your Life (Creation)
God created you and loves you. You were created to enjoy a personal relationship with God. Even before God created the foundation of the earth, you were the focus of His love. In fact, you were created in the image of God!

"So God created man in His own image; in the image of God He created him; male and female He created them" Genesis 1:27.

"Blessed be the God and Father of our Lord Jesus Christ, who has blessed us with every spiritual blessing in the heavenly places in Christ, just as He chose us in Him before the foundation of the world, that we should be holy and without blame before Him in love" (Ephesians 1:3-4).

Our Problem is Sin (The Fall)
That special relationship with God was broken because of sin. God did not make us robots to mindlessly love and obey Him. Instead, He gave us a will and freedom to choose. But we often choose to disobey God and go our own selfish way. This is called sin. Sin separates us from God and causes us to live our lives outside of His will.

"For all have sinned and fall short of the glory of God" Romans 3:23.

"But your iniquities have separated you from your God; your sins have hidden his face from you, so that he will not hear" Isaiah 59:2.

Our sin separates us from God. It keeps us from realizing God's purpose for us and denies us the ability to have a relationship with God.

God's Remedy is Jesus (Redemption)
Jesus Christ is the only answer to this problem of sin and separation from God. He died on the cross and rose from the grave to pay the penalty for our sin. He completely bridges the gap between God and us. Therefore, we need forgiveness of our sin in order to have a relationship with God.

"But God demonstrates his own love for us in this: while we were still sinners, Christ died for us" Romans 5:8.

"Salvation is found in no one else, for there is no other name under heaven given to men by which we must be saved" Acts 4:12.

"God is on one side and all the people on the other side, and Christ Jesus, himself man, is between them to bring them together, by giving his life for all mankind" 1 Timothy 2:5-6.

"I tell you the truth, whoever hears my word and believes him who sent me has eternal life and will not be condemned; he has crossed over from death to life" John 5:24.

God has promised the only way to salvation and Heaven is through Jesus Christ, and we must make the choice to accept Christ as God's remedy for our sin problem.

We Must Respond (Restoration)
When you accept Christ as your Savior, the Holy Spirit works within you to make you more Christ-like in character. You will continue to sin and make mistakes, but the Holy Spirit works within you to help you grow in spiritual maturity. One day you will be fully restored and get to meet Christ face-to-face and spend eternity with Him in heaven. Those who never accepted Christ will continue to be separated from God into eternity.

"All the prophets testify about him that everyone who believes in him receives forgiveness of sins through his name" Acts 10:43.

"Yet to all who received him, to those who believed in his name, he gave the right to become children of God" John 1:12.

How to receive Christ as your Savior:
1. Admit your need (I am a sinner).
2. Believe that Jesus Christ died for you on the cross and rose from the grave. He did this to pay the debt for your sin. This means that we can ask Jesus to forgive us of our sins!
3. Confess Jesus Christ as Lord by inviting Him to come in and control your life.

Here is an example of what to pray:
Dear Jesus, Thank you for making me and loving me (CREATION), even when I've ignored You and gone my own way (THE FALL). I realize I need You in my life and I'm sorry for my sins. I ask You to forgive me. Thank You for dying on the cross for me (REDEMPTION). Please help me to understand it more. As much as I know how, I want to follow You from now on. Please come into my life and make me a new person inside. I accept Your gift of salvation. Please help me to grow now as a Christian (RESTORATION). Amen.

APPENDIX B:

LifeChange: New Believer Devotional

A Letter from Pastor Chris to New Believers
Dear Friend,

Congratulations! You have made the most important commitment a person can ever make! Accepting Jesus Christ as your personal Lord and Savior impacts your life now and for eternity. The life-change that you have experienced is what the Bible calls a new birth. When you were physically born, you came into the world as a baby and then grew into maturity. The same is true of your spiritual birth; you need to grow into spiritual maturity. It is our desire, as your church family, to assist you in growing spiritually.

This handbook will help you get started on your spiritual growth journey. During the first seven days we will give you a brief introduction to seven beginning steps for new believers. It is important to follow through on all of these devotions as they will give you a strong biblical foundation for your faith journey. I have discovered through many years of following Christ that wherever there is divine operation there will be demonic opposition. In other words, whenever God works in our hearts and we respond in obedience (i.e. divine operation) we are going to face obstacles and challenges that will attempt to stop us from growing in our faith (i.e. demonic opposition). Your salvation is secure in Christ and has been sealed by the Holy Spirit. However, Satan does not want you to mature in your faith and continue the mission in which Jesus has entrusted to His followers.

Please know that you have been prayed for! We know that you will need help as you begin living your life for Christ. God has given you a spiritual family to help you mature in your faith. The church is not *like* a family, the church *is* a family; and we're here for you!

Celebrating your decision!

Pastor Chris

P.S.
Before jumping into the handbook, here are a couple of things you may want to do...

1. Have you signed up for baptism?
2. Have you completed CLASS 101?

LifeChange: Introduction

As you begin to work through this week of devotions, let me encourage you to write down questions you might discover along the way. When I first became a Christian I was embarrassed that I couldn't find Scripture passages as fast as others. There is no reason to feel like you should have your Bible's Table of Contents (ToC) memorized. The ToC is there for a reason... use it!

Here is a quick crash course in Scripture references...

The Bible consists of 66 different books. Those books are grouped into two major divisions: The Old Testament (39 books) and the New Testament (27 books). The ultimate connection between the Testaments is that the Old Testament is a prediction of Jesus Christ and the New Testament is the fulfillment through Jesus Christ. When we reference a particular verse of the Bible we list the name of the book followed by a set of two numbers. For example: John 3:16. Using our Table of Contents we notice there are several books named John (i.e. John, 1 John, 2 John, and 3 John). We discover the "John" in our example is referring to the Gospel According to John in the New Testament. The "3" refers to the chapter and the "16" refers to the verse.

Here are a few other considerations as you prepare to work through this handbook...

1. Get a Bible to use with this handbook. There are various translations of the Bible. These translations are not different Bibles, the translators are simply trying to translate the original languages (Hebrew, Greek, and Aramaic) into English in the most understandable way. Some translators focus on a word- for-word translation and others focus on a thought-for-thought translation. The KJV, NKJV, and ESV are all examples of word-for-word translations. The NIV, NLT, and CEV are examples of thought-for-thought translations. I often use both the NKJV and NLT in helping me understand what the Bible passage is saying. NOTE: It is best to memorize from a word-for-word translation.

2. Get a pen or pencil for taking notes and answering the questions. Write down your own questions for further study and discussion in your small group.

3. In part, the purpose of this 7-day study is to help you discover truths from God's word (The Bible). As you read each question, turn to the Scripture reference in your personal Bible and search for the answer.

4. As you read God's word in search of the answers, keep in mind that there are no "trick questions." The questions are intended to be direct and the answers will be found directly from Scripture. The primary purpose of this personal learning tool is to encourage your personal walk with Christ and to help you mature in your faith.

Step 1: Assurance of Your Salvation

God wants you to have confidence that your salvation is secure. As you already know, salvation is a gift that you cannot earn. Our understanding of the security of your salvation is not based upon feelings, but based upon the facts discovered from God's word.

1. **Your Assurance Is Based on the Word of God.** The Bible makes it clear in John 3:16 as well as 1 John 5:11-13 that God wants you to know that you have eternal life. Take a moment and read these two Bible verses and highlight/underline them in your Bible.

2. **Your Assurance is Based on the Promises of God.** In the space provided below, read Romans 10:9 and John 5:24 and then write down the promises found in these verses.

    Romans 10:9   _____
    John 5:24   _____

3. **Your Assurance Is Based on the Character of God.** A promise is only as reliable as the person who makes it. That is why the assurance of your salvation rests on God's character. What do these verses teach about God's character?

    1 Corinthians 1:9   _____
    1 Thessalonians 5:24   _____
    Hebrews 10:23   _____

The Bible teaches that God is faithful (reliable, steadfast, trustworthy, and stable). You can believe the promises because you know the Promisor. God, your loving Father, is absolutely faithful. Nothing will change His mind about your salvation. Nothing will separate you from His love. Your relationship to God through Jesus Christ is secure.

What does God's word say about the security of your salvation? Read Romans 8:38-39. Can any circumstance separate you from God?

4. **Your Assurance Is Based on the Spirit of God.** To further assure you of your salvation, God has sent living, daily proof of your relationship. As an official seal is placed on a contract between two individuals to guarantee the contract's validity, so God has given a seal (guarantee) of His promise to you.

Read Ephesians 1:13-13. What is the seal given by God as a guarantee of His promise? _____

The Holy Spirit at work within you is indisputable proof of your salvation. The Holy Spirit's work in your life will bring changes. Some changes will be gradual; some will be instant. The inward and outward changes that result are evidence of your salvation.

Step 1 Review

- Read 2 Corinthians 5:17.

- What changes have you seen in your life since you committed it to Jesus Christ?

  _____
  _____
  _____

- Don't forget that your assurance is based on:
  1. The _____ of God.
  2. The _____ of God.
  3. The _____ of God.
  4. The _____ of God.

Congratulations! You have completed the first devotion.

Step 2: Publicly Declare Your Faith

After you make a commitment to trust Jesus as your Lord and Savior, it is important for you to take the first step of obedience to Christ and follow Him in baptism.

1. **Why Should I Be Baptized?** A test of whether a person is a true follower of Jesus Christ is his or her obedience to Jesus' commands.
   A. **To follow the example set by Christ.** (Read the account of Jesus' baptism in Matthew 3:13-17).
   B. **Because Christ commanded it.** (Read Matthew 28:19-20.) Baptism is not a suggestion or an option for His followers. If we are not baptized, we are disobedient.
   C. **It is a public testimony of your faith in Christ.** (Read Matthew 10:32.) Therefore, baptism is an act of obedience that publicly declares one's faith.

2. **What is the Meaning of Baptism?** Baptism is a picture of two things: what Jesus did for you and what has happened to you.
   A. **Baptism illustrates Jesus' death, burial, and resurrection.** (Read 1 Corinthians 15:3-4).
   B. **Baptism illustrates my death to sin, the burial of my old self, as well as my new life as a Christian** (Read Romans 6:4.) Remember that baptism doesn't make you a Believer; it demonstrates that you already believe. It's important to understand that baptism does not save you. You are saved only by grace through faith in Jesus. (Read Ephesians 2:8-9)

3. **Why Be Baptized By Immersion?**
   A. **Because Jesus was baptized that way.** (Read Matthew 3:13-17).
   B. **Because every baptism in the Bible was by immersion.**
   C. **Because the word "baptize" actually means "to dip under water."** The Greek word "baptizo" means "to fully immerse or dip under water."
   D. **Because immersion best symbolizes a burial and resurrection!**

4. **Who Should Be Baptized?** Every person who has believed in Christ should be baptized. (Read Acts 2:41)

5. **When Should I Be Baptized?** As soon as you have believed!

There is no reason to delay. As soon as you have decided to receive Christ into your life, you can and should be baptized at your earliest opportunity. If you wait until you are "perfect" you'll never be ready.

If you have not been baptized, you can sign up by calling the church offices at 859.498.5645.

Step 2 Review

- Based on what you just read, fill in the blanks...
  1. Baptism is a public _____ of your faith in Christ.
  2. Baptism is a picture of Jesus' death, _____, and resurrection.
  3. Baptism is a picture of my death to sin, the burial of my old self, as well as my _____ _____ as a Christian.
  4. The word "baptize" actually means "to _____ _____ water."
  5. Every person who has _____ should be baptized.

Fantastic! You've completed the second devotion.

Step 3: Join a Small Group

You were not created to live life in isolation from others. God has created you to live in community with other believers. Joining a Small Group is a crucial step for your continued spiritual growth. God has placed individuals in families for their care, protection, encouragement, and development. You need your church family for the same reasons (and many more). Consider these biblical reasons for joining a small group.

1. **You need healthy Christian relationships for care and support.**
   Take a moment and read Ecclesiastes 4:9-10. What is one of the benefits of being in a small group according to God's word?

   _____

   _____

   _____

   _____

2. **You need healthy Christian relationships for encouragement.**
   Take a moment and read Hebrews 10:24-25. Why do you need the fellowship of a small group?

   _____

   _____

   _____

   _____

3. **You need healthy Christian relationships for instruction.**
   Take a moment and read Ephesians 4:1-16. What is the role of leaders in the church (v.12)? What is the role of all believers (saints v.12)? What is the result when everyone works together (v.16)?

   _____

   _____

   _____

   _____

Step 3 Review

- Why do you believe it is important for you to join a small group?

  _____
  _____
  _____
  _____

- Have you joined a small group? If so, write down a snapshot of your group...
  1. Leader(s)?   _____
  2. When?   _____
  3. Where   _____

- Spend some time in prayer for those in your small group.

- As much as you need your small group, your small group needs you! If you have not joined a small group, contact the church offices and we can help you find the right group!

You're doing great! You've completed the third devotion.

Step 4: Develop Spiritual Disciplines

We will explain Spiritual HABITS in greater detail during CLASS 102. In the meantime, it is important to know that developing spiritual disciplines is an important part of your faith journey. Here are six spiritual disciplines that we encourage every believer to develop...

- Hang Time with God (Daily Bible Readying & Prayer)
- Accountability in a Small Group
- Bible Memorization
- Involvement in the Ministry & Mission of the Church
- Tithing/Stewardship Commitment
- Sermon Application

It is important for new believers to begin immediately developing the discipline of daily Bible reading and prayer. Read 2 Timothy 3:16 and then reach each of the following benefits of reading God's Word.

1. **God's Word is useful for doctrine.** Reading God's word can teach us about our faith.
   Take a moment and read Jeremiah 31:3. What does this passage teach you about God?

   _____

   _____

   Take a moment and read Romans 5:8. What does this passage teach you about God?

   _____

   _____

2. **God's Word is useful for reproof/rebuking.** Reading God's word can point out a fault and the Holy Spirit brings conviction.
   Take a moment and read Ephesians 4:26-31. What are some areas in this passage that God's word gives us guidance?

   _____

   _____

3. **God's Word is useful for correction.** The Bible doesn't just point out what we are doing wrong, but gives us guidance for living life God's way.
   Write out the answer to the question that is presented in Psalm 119:9.

   _____

   _____

4. **God's Word is useful for instruction in righteousness.** Reading God's

word is spiritual food for your soul. Just as your physical body requires nutrients from the food you eat, your spiritual life requires the daily reading nutrients of God's word.

Take a moment and read Jeremiah 15:16. What do you think is meant by this passage?

_____

_____

Step 4 Review

- What are the six Spiritual HABITS?

  H _____
  A _____
  B _____
  I   _____
  T _____
  S _____

- What are the four benefits of reading God's word?
  1. God's word is useful for _____.
  2. God's word is useful for _____.
  3. God's word is useful for _____.
  4. God's word is useful for _____.

Keep up the great work! You've completed the fourth devotion.

Step 5: Become Others Focused

The Christian faith is not a self-centered faith. As we become more like Christ, our concern for others should increase. One of the ways that we express our love for one another is through serving on ministry teams.

The Bible teaches that every believer has a role to serve within the body of Christ (cf. 1 Corinthians 12). What God made me to be determines what He intends for me to do. God is consistent in His plan for each of our lives. He would not give us spiritual gifts, passions, talents, temperaments, and all sorts of experiences and then not want to use them for His glory! We will explore these five personal factors in detail during CLASS 103.

A huge indication of spiritual maturity is when you take off the bib and you put on the apron. Instead of saying things like, "I'm not being fed" the mature believer says, "What am I doing to feed others?" Here are three key truths as to why we should serve the needs of others:

1. **Serving the needs of others reflects the mind of Christ.**
   Read Philippians 2:1-5. How can you begin to put the needs of others ahead of your own?

   _____

   _____

2. **Serving the needs of others produces increased fruitfulness.**
   Read 2 Peter 1:5-9. What are some of the characteristics that produce a fruitful walk with Christ?

   _____

   _____

3. **Serving the needs of others is a testimony of Jesus' love for others.**
   Read John 13:34-35. What is the identifier of a true disciple according to this passage?

   _____

   _____

Step 5 Review

- What are some of the ways that you can begin to focus on others...

  ...at home?   _____

  ...at work/school?   _____

  ...in my neighborhood?   _____

- Fill in the blanks: "A huge indication of spiritual maturity is when you take off the _____ and you put on the _____." Write down in your own words what this phrase means...

  _____
  _____
  _____
  _____

You're almost there! You've completed the fifth devotion.

Step 6: Share Jesus with Others

People love to share good news. We announce marriages and births. When something good happens, we rush to tell someone. The more exciting the news, the harder it is to be silent.

A Christian has the most exciting news – the life-changing news of eternal life! It is natural for a Christian to want to share this good news. Think for a moment about the various people God used to bring you to the place where you were willing to receive Jesus.

Now God wants you to be part of helping others come to know Jesus.

When Andrew met Jesus, his first inclination was to bring _____ to meet Him (read John 1:40-42).

For a Christian, witnessing is not an option. Jesus commanded His followers to witness.

There are two tools you should use when sharing Jesus:

- Scripture
- Your Personal Testimony

1. **Scripture**
   The following verses will help you explain to unbelievers the good news of eternal life. Take time now to read them and underline/highlight them in your Bible. It would be good to memorize them too!
   - Romans 15:13
   - Romans 1:16
   - Romans 2:4
   - Romans 3:23
   - Romans 5:8
   - Romans 6:23
   - Romans 10:9-13

2. **Your Personal Testimony**
   A. **Salvation Testimony:** Your salvation testimony shares (1) your life before receiving Jesus, (2) how you received Jesus, and (3) how Jesus is making a difference in your life now.
   B. **Growth Testimony:** You will have many growth testimonies as you mature in your faith. Your growth testimonies share (1) an issue or question you've been struggling with, (2) the lesson you learned about the issue/question from studying Scripture, and (3) how you have responded to God's word in light of what you learned.

Take some time to write out your personal salvation testimony. Make sure you include all three parts: life before receiving Jesus, how you received Jesus, and how Jesus is working in your life now.

We cover these testimonies in more detail in CLASS 104. You can also pick up the resource called "Everyone Has a Story," available in the church's Resource Center. Until then, you can begin to share Jesus by simply inviting others to attend worship services with you.

Step 6 Review

• Why should you share Jesus with others?

_____

_____

_____

_____

• Whom do you know who needs to receive Jesus?

_____

_____

_____

_____

• Share your testimony with someone this week.

You're almost finished! You've completed the sixth devotion.

Step 7: Trust Jesus Daily

The Christian faith is more than fire insurance to save you from hell. It is a daily walk with our Creator and living a fulfilled life as God intended.

As you mature in your faith, you will discover more and more what it means to "surrender your life to Christ" and "live for Him."

1. **Jesus Christ has earned the right to give you direction.**
    [Jesus] "... humbled Himself and became obedient to the point of death, even the death of the _____. Therefore God also has highly exalted Him and given Him the name which is above every name, that at the name of _____ every knee should bow, of those in heaven, and of those on earth, and of those under the earth, and that every tongue should confess that _____ _____ is _____, to the glory of God the Father" Philippians 2:5-8.

    Paul (the author of the book of Philippians), understood that Jesus was worthy to direct his life.

    Paul also challenged believers to do what in Romans 12:1-2?
    _____
    _____

2. **Jesus Christ desires to give you direction.**
    Many people want to know God's will and He desires to reveal it daily through time spent with Him. His direction can be experienced on a daily basis as you:

    A. Recognize daily His right to direct you life (read Luke 9:23).
    B. Confess your sins and accept His promise of forgiveness (read 1 John 1:9).
    C. Trust Him completely as you allow Him to direct your:
        ❑ Time (read Ephesians 5:15-16)
        ❑ Money (read 1 Corinthians 16:2)
        ❑ Abilities (read Colossians 3:17)
        ❑ Relationships (read Matthew 22:34-40)
        ❑ Mind (read Romans 12:1-2)
        ❑ Ambitions (read Matthew 6:33)
        ❑ Morality (read 1 Corinthians 6:19-20)

Step 7 Review

- What areas in your life need to be placed under the direction of Jesus? Don't delay. I always told my son, "Delayed obedience is disobedience."
  - ✓ Time:　　　　　_____
  - ✓ Money:　　　　_____
  - ✓ Relationships:　_____
  - ✓ Mind:　　　　　_____
  - ✓ Ambitions:　　　_____
  - ✓ Morality:　　　 _____

Congratulations! Now that you have completed the seven beginning steps, you are ready to continue to develop them more fully.

Your next steps...
Complete
- ❑ CLASS 101
- ❑ CLASS 102
- ❑ CLASS 103
- ❑ CLASS 104

APPENDIX C:
Spiritual Gifts Inventory

Directions:
Using the Spiritual Gifts Grid found in this section, enter the numerical value that best describes to what extent the statement accurately describes you. Do not answer on the basis of what you wish were true, but on the basis of what to your knowledge is true of you. When you are finished, add up the six numbers that you have recorded in each row and place the sum in the "total" column. Use the following numeric values...

3 = **Much**

2 = **Some**

1 = **Little**

0 = **Not at all**

1. I could be described as an "others-centered" person.

2. I believe I have the gift of helping.

3. I enjoy giving hope to those in need.

4. When people are in need I enjoy having them in my home. I do not feel like they are intruding.

5. I believe I have the gift of exhortation.

6. I see myself as a person who is very generous when it comes to giving money to my church.

7. My friends view me as a person who is wise.

8. I have expressed thoughts of truth that have given insight to others.

9. I often feel I know God's will even when others aren't sure.

10. I would like to be a missionary.

11. I can tell nonbelievers about my relationship with Christ in a comfortable manner.

12. I enjoy explaining biblical truths to people.

13. I have a way of relating to and comforting those who have fallen away from the Lord.

14. I believe I know where I am going and other people seem to follow.

15. I see clearly that a job can be done more effectively if I allow others to assist.

16. I enjoy meeting the needs of others.

17. I'm the one who often cleans up after the meeting without being asked.

18. I believe I have the gift of mercy.

19. I enjoy having strangers in my home. I like making them feel comfortable.

20. I believe I have the ability to comfort those who are "off-track" and help them get back on track.

21. I believe I have the gift of giving.

22. I believe God has given me the ability to make wise decisions.

23. I desire fully to understand biblical truths.

24. I enjoy helping others with spiritual needs.

25. I feel comfortable when I'm around people of a different culture, race, or language.

26. I believe I have the gift of evangelism.

27. I think I have what it takes to teach a Bible study or lead a small group discussion.

28. I try to know people in a personal way so that we feel comfortable with one another.

29. I would enjoy leading, inspiring, and motivating others to become involved in God's work.

30. I would enjoy directing a vacation Bible school, recreation program or special event for my church.

31. You'll frequently find me volunteering my time to help with the needs of the church.

32. I seldom think twice before doing a task that might not bring me praise.

33. I would like to visit rest homes and other institutions where people need visitors.

34. I believe I have the gift of hospitality.

35. I have a desire to learn more about counseling so I can help others.

36. I have a strong desire to use my money wisely, knowing God will direct my giving.

37. I believe God has blessed me with the gift of wisdom.

38. I am able to help others understand God's Word.

39. I find it easy to trust God in difficult situations.

40. I adapt easily to a change of settings.

41. I have the ability to direct conversations toward the message of Christ.

42. I am willing to spend extra time studying biblical principles in order to communicate them clearly to others.

43. I would like the responsibilities that my pastor has.

44. I want to lead people to the best solution when they have troubles.

45. I can give others responsibilities for a task or project and help them accomplish it.

46. I'm the type of person that likes to reach out to less fortunate people.

47. I receive joy doing jobs that others see as "thankless."

48. I am very compassionate to those in need.

49. I believe God has given me the ability to make others feel comfortable in my home.

50. I have helped others in their struggles.

51. I am confident that God will take care of my needs when I give sacrificially and cheerfully.

52. I feel confident that my decisions are in harmony with God's will.

53. I believe I have the gift of knowledge.

54. I trust in God for supernatural miracles.

55. I have a strong desire to see people in other countries won to the Lord.

56. I have led others to a personal relationship with Christ.

57. I believe I have the gift of teaching.

58. I would like to be a pastor.

59. I have influenced others to complete a task or to find a biblical answer that helped their lives.

60. I am able to set goals and plan the most effective way to reach them.

61. I feel good when I help with the routine jobs at the church.

62. I am able to do jobs that others won't do and I feel good about myself.

63. I have a desire to work with people who have special physical needs.

64. I want my house to always be a spot where people in need can come and find rest.

65. I enjoy seeing people respond to encouragement.

66. I am a cheerful giver of my money.

67. I usually see clear solutions to complicated problems.

68. I have the ability to learn new insights on my own.

69. I believe I have the gift of faith.

70. I am willing to go wherever God want to send me.

71. I desire to learn more about God so I can share Him in a more clear way.

72. Others tell me I present the gospel in a way that is easy to understand.

73. When I teach from the Bible my concern is that I see results in the spiritual growth of others.

74. I believe I have leadership skills.

75. I enjoy learning about management issues and how organizations function.

76. I believe I have the gift of serving.

77. You'll often find me volunteering to do "behind the scenes" activities that few notice but must be done.

78. I would like to have a ministry with those who are needy.

79. I enjoy providing food and housing to those in need.

80. I am known for the way I encourage others.

81. I enjoy giving money to the needy.

82. God has given me the ability to give clear counsel and advice to others.

83. I tend to use biblical insights when I share with others.

84. Others in my group see me as a faithful Christian.

85. I believe I could learn a new language well enough to minister to those in a different culture.

86. I always think of new ways in which I can share Christ with my non-Christian friends.

87. Because of my teaching, I have brought others to a better understanding of the Christian faith.

88. I can see myself taking responsibility for the spiritual growth of others.

89. When I'm in a group I'm usually the leader or I take the lead if no one else does.

90. I believe I have the gift of administration.

Spiritual Gifts Grid:

Rows:	Value of Answers:						Total:
A	1 _____	16 _____	31 _____	46 _____	61 _____	76 _____	_____
B	2 _____	17 _____	32 _____	47 _____	62 _____	77 _____	_____
C	3 _____	18 _____	33 _____	48 _____	63 _____	78 _____	_____
D	4 _____	19 _____	34 _____	49 _____	64 _____	79 _____	_____
E	5 _____	20 _____	35 _____	50 _____	65 _____	80 _____	_____
F	6 _____	21 _____	36 _____	51 _____	66 _____	81 _____	_____
G	7 _____	22 _____	37 _____	52 _____	67 _____	82 _____	_____
H	8 _____	23 _____	38 _____	53 _____	68 _____	83 _____	_____
I	9 _____	24 _____	39 _____	54 _____	69 _____	84 _____	_____
J	10 _____	25 _____	40 _____	55 _____	70 _____	85 _____	_____
K	11 _____	26 _____	41 _____	56 _____	71 _____	86 _____	_____
L	12 _____	27 _____	42 _____	57 _____	72 _____	87 _____	_____
M	13 _____	28 _____	43 _____	58 _____	73 _____	88 _____	_____
N	14 _____	29 _____	44 _____	59 _____	74 _____	89 _____	_____
O	15 _____	30 _____	45 _____	60 _____	75 _____	90 _____	_____

Application:

When you are finished, add up the six numbers that you have recorded in each row and place the sum in the "total" column. Now using the corresponding letter from each row (using the chart on the next page), identify your top three spiritual gifts. This is your gift mix. Don't just look at your strongest gift; study how these gifts relate to one another.

1. _____

2. _____

3. _____

Spiritual Gifts:

Row A	Serving
Row B	Helping
Row C	Mercy
Row D	Hospitality
Row E	Exhortation
Row F	Giving
Row G	Wisdom
Row H	Knowledge
Row I	Faith
Row J	Missionary
Row K	Evangelism
Row L	Teaching
Row M	Pastoring
Row N	Leadership
Row O	Administration

APPENDIX D:
2020 Vision

1. We have a vision for reaching 10% of the population of Mount Sterling, Kentucky!
2. We have a vision for being debt free and developing a master plan for the existing main campus!
3. We have a vision for launching 40 satellite campuses in each of the 40 counties of eastern Kentucky (those east of I-75). We would like to see the first four of those fully operational by 2020 and each campus' goal is to reach 10% of their county.
4. We have a vision for developing a staff at the main campus that will serve as a resource for all satellite campuses. For example, our student pastor equips the satellite student pastors and develops a network for student ministry. Likewise, our worship pastor equips the satellite worship pastors and develops a network for worship ministry. Children's ministry resources, student ministry resources, worship ministry resources, discipleship resources, and more will be developed.

40-Day Spiritual Growth Campaigns
Other Books Available in the Series

These and other resources are available on Amazon.

40 Days of Prayer (Released 2015)
"40 Days of Prayer" is a 40-day study of the Lord's Model Prayer (i.e. Matthew 6:8-13).

40 Days of Love (Released 2016)
"40 Days of Love" is a 40-day study of 1 Corinthians 13.

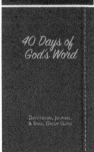

40 Days of God's Word (Released 2017)
"40 Days of God's Word" is a 40-day study of Psalm 119.

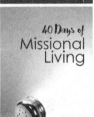

40 Days of Missional Living (Released 2018)
"40 Days of Missional Living" is a 40-day study of the Great Commission.

Coming 2019: 40 Days of Stewardship
Coming 2020: 40 Days of Worship

Made in the USA
Las Vegas, NV
11 October 2022

57021322R00105